THE WRECKER

by Arnold Ridley
and Bernard Merivale

∥SAMUEL FRENCH∥

Copyright © 1930 by Samuel French Ltd
All Rights Reserved

THE WRECKER is fully protected under the copyright laws of the British Commonwealth, including Canada, the United States of America, and all other countries of the Copyright Union. All rights, including professional and amateur stage productions, recitation, lecturing, public reading, motion picture, radio broadcasting, television, online/digital production, and the rights of translation into foreign languages are strictly reserved.

ISBN 978-0-573-00023-2

concordtheatricals.co.uk
concordtheatricals.com

FOR AMATEUR PRODUCTION ENQUIRIES

UNITED KINGDOM AND WORLD
EXCLUDING NORTH AMERICA
licensing@concordtheatricals.co.uk
020-7054-7298

Each title is subject to availability from Concord Theatricals, depending upon country of performance.

CAUTION: Professional and amateur producers are hereby warned that *THE WRECKER* is subject to a licensing fee. The purchase, renting, lending or use of this book does not constitute a licence to perform this title(s), which licence must be obtained from the appropriate agent prior to any performance. Performance of this title(s) without a licence is a violation of copyright law and may subject the producer and/or presenter of such performances to penalties. Both amateurs and professionals considering a production are strongly advised to apply to the appropriate agent before starting rehearsals, advertising, or booking a theatre. A licensing fee must be paid whether the title is presented for charity or gain and whether or not admission is charged.

This work is published by Samuel French, an imprint of Concord Theatricals Ltd.

The Professional Rights in this play are controlled by AGENT INFO AND ADDRESS.

No one shall make any changes in this title for the purpose of production. No part of this book may be reproduced, stored in a retrieval system, scanned, uploaded, or transmitted in any form, by any means, now known or yet to be invented, including mechanical, electronic, digital, photocopying, recording, videotaping, or otherwise, without the prior written permission of the publisher. No one shall share this title, or part of this title, to any social media or file hosting websites.

The moral right of Arnold Ridley and Bernard Merivale to be identified as author of this work has been asserted in accordance with Section 77 of the Copyright, Designs and Patents Act 1988.

USE OF COPYRIGHTED MUSIC

A licence issued by Concord Theatricals to perform this play does not include permission to use the incidental music specified in this publication. In the United Kingdom: Where the place of performance is already licensed by the PERFORMING RIGHT SOCIETY (PRS) a return of the music used must be made to them. If the place of performance is not so licensed then application should be made to PRS for Music (www.prsformusic.com). A separate and additional licence from PHONOGRAPHIC PERFORMANCE LTD (www.ppluk.com) may be needed whenever commercial recordings are used. Outside the United Kingdom: Please contact the appropriate music licensing authority in your territory for the rights to any incidental music.

USE OF COPYRIGHTED THIRD-PARTY MATERIALS

Licensees are solely responsible for obtaining formal written permission from copyright owners to use copyrighted third-party materials (e.g., artworks, logos) in the performance of this play and are strongly cautioned to do so. If no such permission is obtained by the licensee, then the licensee must use only original materials that the licensee owns and controls. Licensees are solely responsible and liable for clearances of all third-party copyrighted materials, and shall indemnify the copyright owners of the play(s) and their licensing agent, Concord Theatricals Ltd., against any costs, expenses, losses and liabilities arising from the use of such copyrighted third-party materials by licensees.

IMPORTANT BILLING AND CREDIT REQUIREMENTS

If you have obtained performance rights to this title, please refer to your licensing agreement for important billing and credit requirements.

THE WRECKER

Produced at the New Theatre, St. Martin's Lane, London, on Tuesday, December 6th, 1927. The cast was as follows

(In the order of their appearance.)

MILLY KNIGHT	Ivy Sparrow
GLADYS ELLIOTT	Norah Howard
MARY SHELTON	Edna Davies
NOAH TWEMBLETT	Frank Bertram
ROGER DOYLE	G. H. Mulcaster
JOSHUA BARNEY	George Elton
SIR GERVAISE BARTLETT	Owen Roughwood
A CLERK	Vaughan Powel
INSPECTOR RATOHETT	Vincent Holman
LADY BERYL METOHLEY	Fabia Drake
CHESTER KYLE	Keneth Kent
ALFRED	Arthur Young
HORACE SKEET	Herbert Moss
HAINES	Vaughan Powel
JOHN SMITH	J. Adrian Byrne

Play produced by Sewell Collins

CHARACTERS

MILLY KNIGHT – Ivy Sparrow
GLADYS ELLIOTT – Norah Howard
MARY SHELTON – Edna Davies
NOAH TWEMBLETT – Frank Bertram
ROGER DOYLE – G. H. Mulcaster
JOSHUA BARNEY – George Elton
SIR GERVAISE BARTLETT – Owen Roughwood
A CLERK – Vaughan Powel
INSPECTOR RATOHETT – (of the Railway Police) Vincent Holman
LADY BERYL METOHLEY – Fabia Drake
CHESTER KYLE – Keneth Kent
ALFRED – Arthur Young
HORACE SKEET – Herbert Moss
HAINES – Vaughan Powel
JOHN SMITH – J. Adrian Byrne

SETTING

ACT ONE
The General Office of the Great Trunk Railway.

ACT TWO
Scene One The Library of Roger's House in Marylebone Square.
Scene Two – A signal box.

ACT THREE
The General Office of the Great Trunk Railway (Same as Act I).

ACT ONE

(Scene – The General Office of the Great Trunk Railway. It is a large room furnished with desks, typewriters, etc. The back wall contains two windows, diagonally set at corners which, the office being on the first floor of the London terminus, look out on to the line. When trains leave, their steam can be seen rising outside the window. In the distance can be seen very faintly several signal gantries and the red and green lights of the distant signals. Down left there is a door leading to a smaller office. And, opposite down right, another door opening from corridor. This is the main entrance to the room. Between the windows, in back wall is the train indicator, about eight feet long by two and a half feet high, three or four inches in thickness. This rests on wainscoting two feet nine inches from floor. There are two flat-topped office desks below each window, their chairs above them with back to windows. The desk at left is **BARNEY**'s *desk. It is covered with papers and on it a green-shaded desk lamp. On the right desk are other papers. Wastepaper basket under* **BARNEY**'s *desk. At back, under indicator, a long table, a card-index file with drawers up right of desk right. Against right wall a table with papers. In front (below) desk right and an office chair down extreme right. A small chair – as well as one down extreme left side. Against the left wall above door left a typist's*

desk with typewriter and chair. On walls around room are posters, railway pictures, prints of engines, trains, etc. And on wall up left is a portrait (about fourteen by sixteen inches) of **SIR GERVAISE BARTLETT** – *to fall at cue.)*

(When the curtain rises it is about three thirty p.m. on a December afternoon and the light is bad. The stage is empty. A train is heard to enter the station underneath. **MILLY** *and* **GLADYS**, *two typists, enter from door right.)*

GLADYS. *(Centre.)* Oh, that infernal din! For God's sake shut the window!

> (**MILLY** *moves up right and shuts window. The noise decreases.)*

Who opened it?

MILLY. Mr. Barney. He says he must ventilate the room when no one's here. *(Putting her coat, etc., on table up centre.)*

GLADYS. Silly old crank! Ventilation! *(Crossing to window left.)* A fat lot of fresh air gets in from the station. Nothing but smuts and steam.

> *(Train noise stops.)*

(Below desk left.) Where's my powder-puff? *(Suddenly.)* Oh, damn!

MILLY. *(Centre.)* What's the matter?

GLADYS. *(Moving to above desk.)* I believe – yes, I have. I've bust the elastic of my knickers again. *(Examining the offending garment.)* Got a safety-pin?

MILLY. *(Centre left, fishing in her bag.)* Here you are. *(Handing* **GLADYS** *the safety-pin.)* Do be *quick*! Suppose Mr. Barney came in.

GLADYS. *(Pinning up her knickers.)* Suppose he did? What of it?

MILLY. Gladys!

GLADYS. *(Moving down to front of desk.)* That man's nothing but a timetable. Just about as human as his train indicator. If I was standing here stark naked when he came in he'd just blink his eyes and murmur, "Saturdays only, change at Doncaster." *(Crossing to right.)*

MILLY. Gladys! You do say *awful* things. I hope you won't talk like that in front of the new girl.

GLADYS. Bah! *(Taking an apple from her pocket and starting to chew it.)* Seen a paper? *(Going to the door down right and calling.)* No-ah!

> *(***GLADYS** *returns to up centre. An old man enters right. It is* **NOAH TWEM-BLETT**, *an old- driver. He has an artificial arm.)*

NOAH. *(Down right.)* What's up?

> *(***MILLY** *moves to front of desk left.)*

GLADYS. Got a paper, Gaffer?

NOAH. Ah. But only a picture one. *(Pulling a 'Daily Sketch' out of his pocket.)* Don't know what folks be comin' to these days. Hardly ever see ought but picture papers – not a bit of solid readin' left in any carriage all day.

MILLY. What paper do you like, Noah?

NOAH. *(Crossing up centre to left.)* Give me *The Times* or the *Telegraph*. Somethin' you can cut and come again at. No fripperies. 'Aven't found a 'Times' for weeks now. *(Handing paper to* **MILLY.**)

MILLY. Why don't you buy one?

NOAH. *(Crossing down right.)* Buy one? Me been on the railway forty-seven years and *buy* a paper. *(Turning.)* There's a picture of Mr. Roger in that 'un. *(He hobbles out by the door right.)*

GLADYS. Is there? *(Crossing to right of* **MILLY.***)* Let me see, Milly! Look, there! Oh, isn't he a peach?

MILLY. *(Reading.)* 'Lucky Doyle.' "Lucky Doyle forsakes football for business. After securing thirty International Caps, Mr. Roger Doyle has announced his intention of retiring from serious football and devoting himself to the affairs of the Great Trunk Railway. He is the nephew of the present chairman of the Board. It will be long remembered that on every one of the eleven occasions on which Mr. Doyle captained England, he won the toss for ends."

GLADYS. *(Chanting.)* And *that* was *why* they called him 'Lucky Doyle' – *(To left of desk left.)* and I don't blame them.

> *(While* **MILLY** *has been reading this,* **MARY SHELTON** *has entered from the little office left.)*

Hello, kid! *(To* **MARY** *– brings her centre.)* Why didn't you have lunch with us? No need to be shy.

MARY. No. I had to stop late and finish something for Mr. Roger.

> *(A guard's whistle sounds below.)*

What's that? *(Centre.)*

GLADYS. *(Crossing to desk right.)* Boat express just starting.

> *(The noise of a train leaving below.)*

MARY. Ooh! *(Going up to the window right centre.)* Where does it go?

MILLY. Hollystone Head – three hundred miles non-stop. *(Crossing up centre.)* You'll soon get tired of the station. We all do. *(She gets hat, etc., from table centre, and exits with them left.)*

GLADYS. All except the governor.

MARY. Mr. Barney? *(Behind the desk left.)*

GLADYS. *(Putting her apple on the desk right and sitting on table centre.)* No, kid! *The* governor. Why, old Barney *hates* the place; you ought to hear him when an express goes out just as he's in the middle of one of his calculations for his new timetable. I mean Sir Gervaise. He's always standing at this window watching the trains go out. Queer old buffer, Sir Gervaise. Always at *this* window. Why, if ever I saw him look out the other window, I'd believe the end of the world had come.

> *(**MILLY** re-enters with newspaper and goes to small table left.)*

I say, the boat train's three minutes late leaving. Won't old Barney swear! *(Crossing to above desk right.)*

MARY. I wonder what's made it late?

MILLY. Perhaps they've found something. All the main lines are specially examined before they start.

MARY. *(Moving down centre to left.)* You mean in case – because of all these *accidents* lately?

GLADYS. Accidents! You don't *really* think they're accidents, do you? *(At desk right, looking at papers.)*

MARY. Well – I –

MILLY. Five in five weeks. That can't be accidental. Someone's doing it.

GLADYS. Jack the Wrecker! That's what they call him now.

MARY. Ugh! What a horrible name. *(Slight move down centre to left.)*

GLADYS. There's been no smash on our line so far, and if anything should happen to our South Express we shall know just to the tick when and where it happens. *(Pointing to the train indicator.)*

MARY. *(Turning.)* How?

GLADYS. That's Mr. Barney's invention.

*(**MILLY** moves up left.)*

MARY. *(Looking at it.)* I've been wondering what it was. How does it work?

GLADYS. I dunno; there's a wireless transmitter or something fitted to the train. As the train biffs along it sends out signals that move a green light along that line. See the stations marked? When the *train* stops, *it* stops, and should an accident happen, enough to bust up the transmitter, the alarm rings and the light goes to red. That's the bright idea, I believe.

*(**MILLY** moves down to front of desk left.)*

MARY. *(To **GLADYS**.)* You mean if the green light changed to red it would mean there'd been a smash?

GLADYS. You've got it, kid. Mr. Barney's trying it out at present on the South Express. If it comes off they're going to have it rigged up specially for the Rainbow.

MARY. The Rainbow?

GLADYS. Yes, the Great Trunk star train.

MARY. *(Crossing to left.)* I don't like it. I think it's a horrible idea. I'm glad I work in the other office – I should always be looking at it – expecting to hear the alarm and see the red light.

GLADYS. No good worrying. Anyway, nothing's happened to our line so far.

MILLY. Do you know what I think? *(Dropping newspaper on floor below desk.)*

GLADYS. Don't ask *me* to guess, dearie; it's hard enough for you yourself to tell!

MILLY. *(Right of desk left.)* Gladys – aren't you awful! Well, *I* think the real reason Mr. Barney invented the Indicator was not so much to prevent accidents as to keep tabs on the running times.

GLADYS. Milly, you are really threatened with intelligence. *(Pushing* **MILLY** *playfully against* **BARNEY***'s desk, where, she disturbs* **BARNEY***'s papers.)*

MILLY. Look out! Mind Mr. Barney's papers!

GLADYS. Oh lord!

MARY. What *are* all those papers? *(Moving to desk left.)*

GLADYS. Ah, that's the big secret. No one shall touch them! Mr. Barney's new time-table – affectionately known as the T.T.

MILLY. *(Proudly.)* It's got up to fourteen thousand entries and the Western area services not touched yet!

GLADYS. His idea is to make two trains run where only one ran before.

MILLY. By eliminating all lost time – if all the trains kept time you could run more on each track and save thousands a year in expenses.

GLADYS. Yes! And end up in an asylum. *(Crossing to right.)* It's bad enough copying it all out –

    (A bell rings off right.)

That's me, I suppose – no peace for the wicked!

(Taking notebook from her desk right, crossing and colliding with **ROGER** *at door. Exits by door right.)*

"Sorry!"

*(***ROGER** *has entered, a good-looking young fellow. Vigorous 'football' type. He carries a small parcel.)*

ROGER. *(Crossing centre to right. To* **MILLY**.*)* Here's a special registered parcel just come in – most important. Give it to the guard of the South Express, will you? Mr. Barney's O.K.'d it. Hand it to him personally, won't you?

MILLY. *(Crossing to right.)* Yes, sir. If the train's not backed in yet, shall I wait?

ROGER. Yes, please.

*(***MILLY** *goes out by the door right.)*

Sir Gervaise will be in this evening. *(Moving to desk right.)* By Jove! just look at this office! What a state! Just clear it up, Miss Shelton, do you mind?

*(***MARY** *tidies desk left.)*

Whose apple is this?

MARY. *(Crossing to* **ROGER**.*)* I don't know, Mr. Doyle. *(Putting the apple in a wastepaper basket and picking up and folding the newspaper.)* Oh, I say!

ROGER. What is it? *(At desk right.)*

MARY. *(Seeing picture in paper.)* Your photograph in the "Daily Sketch," Mr. Doyle. I suppose you've seen it. *(Moving to centre.)*

ROGER. No. *(Waving away the paper.)* For Heaven's sake, take it away.

>(**MARY** *moves to desk left, takes the paper and after surreptitiously tearing out the photo, puts it in the wastepaper basket left.*)

I want to forget about footer now.

MARY. Is it true you're never going to play again?

ROGER. Not in any important matches. I won't do things by halves. I haven't the time for work *and* footer, and footer's had a good innings. It goes hard, though.

MARY. I'm sure it must. *(In front of desk left.)*

ROGER. One's got to chuck it *sometime. (Moving round front of desk right.)* But I should have loved to go on that New Zealand tour.

MARY. I always think you played your finest game against the New Zealanders at Twick.

ROGER. Twick? What do you know about the game against the New Zealanders?

MARY. I was there.

ROGER. The devil you were – I mean – you follow Rugger, then?

MARY. Rather! I always feel that if Shedley had gone for the line more instead of continually punting ahead, England would have won that match. I shall never forget the last five minutes – you know, when you broke clean away from the line out. You handed off their 'half', and turned in towards the centre.

ROGER. I wanted to cut out an opening for Matthews – he was spoiling for a run.

MARY. And then you decided to go on yourself.

ROGER. I saw Matthews was too heavily marked.

MARY. You swerved out to the left again.

ROGER. Yes. You see, I had their threes on the wrong diagonal.

MARY. I never knew you had such speed – the way you flew down the touch line.

ROGER. I don't know. That wing of theirs, Sedgford, caught me ten yards out.

MARY. I know, and then the full back crashed into you, too. I didn't think you could possibly do it, but you did! Dragged both of them over the line with you – a try!

ROGER. And then Rollenson missed the goal-kick by six inches!

MARY. I know. I could have cried. In fact, I did. *(Turning away down left.)*

ROGER. Strictly between ourselves, so did I – nearly! *(Moving down centre to left.)*

MARY. And then your last game against Scotland, I didn't cry then.

ROGER. Didn't you?

MARY. Oh! I'm sorry, I'm forgetting where I am.

*(**ROGER** crosses away and tidies up the desk right as **MILLY** re-enters from door right.)*

ROGER. *(Centre.)* All right?

MILLY. *(At table right.)* Yes, sir. I found the guard downstairs. *(Sitting at table.)*

ROGER. *(At desk right.)* Good.

*(**GLADYS** enters from door right and goes to desk right.)*

GLADYS. *(Right centre.)* Well, that's that. Three "Dear sirs" and two "Your obedient servants." *(Sitting below desk.)*

*(**ROGER** goes out by the door right.)*

(At desk right.) Hello! Where's my apple?

MARY. *(Centre left.)* In the wastepaper basket.

GLADYS. *(Rising.)* In the where?

MARY. Mr. Doyle told me to throw it away. Sorry.

GLADYS. Like his damn cheek. What does he want, messing about with my apples? Does he think this is the Garden of Eden? *(Diving into the wastepaper basket and retrieving the apple: also the newspaper.)* Hello! Did his nibs remove his pretty picture, too?

MARY. N-no.

GLADYS. *(Pointing to the hole in it.) Somebody* has!

MARY. As a matter of fact – I – I did.

GLADYS. Oho! Milly, we'll have to keep an eye on this child.

MILLY. Yes, I think that a young woman of her age…

MARY. Oh, please don't be silly.

GLADYS. Take my tip, kid, and sheer off. He's booked up already to one of the posh crowd you see every week in the "Tatler" and the "Sketch." You know; lying on the beach at the Ly-do in their pyjamas. *(Crossing to desk right.)*

> *(**NOAH** re-enters from door right with small tool kit.)*

MILLY. What are you going to do with those tools?

> *(**MARY** to table left. Picking up her notebook.)*

NOAH. *(Centre to right.)* Mr. Barney wanted them in case anything went wrong with the new box o' tricks there. *(Pointing to indicator.)* There be a party o' folks comin' to see 'un to-night, and 'er must go off right afore company. *(Moving up centre and putting tools on table centre.)*

(**MARY** *moves down to door left.*)

GLADYS. *(Centre to right.)* Wait a minute, Mary, come and be introduced. *(Winking at* **MILLY**.*)* Noah, this is Bliss Mary Shelton who's come instead of Miss Baynes. And this is Mr. Noah Twemblett who's been in the Great Trunk Company for ever, and is so old that he remembers filling the kettle for Stephenson's mother.

(**GLADYS** *moves to desk right and sits above it.* **MARY** *up to left of* **NOAH**.)

NOAH. *(Centre.)* Pleased to meet you, Miss. Forty-seven year I bin with the Company, man and boy, and fifty-six different injuns I drove, till I lost me arm, and now I be sort of pensioned off to look after things up 'ere in Lunnon office. *(Beginning to fiddle with the indicator.)*

MARY. Forty-seven years? You must have seen some changes.

NOAH. *(Turning.)* Well you may say changes, Miss. I do recollect when the Great North Express took sixteen hours to make Edinburgh and sometimes didn't make it at all when there wur snow or fog. Drivin' *was* drivin' in them days, and little comfort for the driver with the fire o' hell in front of 'im, and Siberia in the small of his back. But, bless you, Miss, changes or no, they're all the same – the old injuns and the new injuns. They know who's on the footplate as well as a norse knows who's in the saddle.

(**GLADYS** *makes signs indicating that* **NOAH** *is feeble-minded.*)

Ah! they knows. There's a three-cylinder super-heated four-four-nought over in the sheds now that no one can do naught with. I wish I could 'ave a cut at un, *I'd* show un. Proper rogue injun that one.

(**GLADYS** *leans against desk right listening,* **MILLY** *listens also.*)

MARY. A rogue engine?

NOAH. Ah! there be rogue injuns, same as rogue 'orses. Why, the only accident I wur ever in – when I lost me arm – she wur a rogue injun. 'Isle of Guernsey' wur 'er name. I knew she'd 'ave me some time or other, and 'ave me she did. Ran into a freighter she did, just this side o' Longton Tunnel. There be a curve this side o' the tunnel and I eased 'er up same as I'd a-done a hundred times or more, but she wouldn't 'ave it. She saw that there freighter on the down track and jumped the rails and ran bang into un.

MARY. Was anyone hurt?

(*The light begins to fail.*)

NOAH. Not a soid, Miss – only me. That there 'Isle o' Guernsey' 'er were *allus* tryin' to get at them freighters.

MARY. But you talk as if the engine was alive.

NOAH. Alive! And who's to say the injuns aren't alive?

GLADYS. Of course they're alive. There's one down there now, smoking!

NOAH. You may joke, Miss, but I *know*. When you makes a thing so powerful, 'ow d'you know it will all end in just the power you give it. Suppose it goes on developing of itself, eh? There's many strange things about injuns, only them knows as 'as druv 'em. Come to the window, Miss.

(*They go to the window left.* **MILLY** *rises, goes to* **GLADYS**.*)*

Look at that 'un down there in Bay number Ten. 'The Queen Mary', two-six-nought. In quarter of an hour she'll be takin' the Rainbow Express up north

– sixty-five miles to the hour, the wind and the rain whistling past 'er – (**NOAH** *moves down centre to left.*) – snow p'raps further up, and all the rich folk sittin' inside smokin' four-penny cigars, which they've paid a shilling for.

(**MILLY** *laughs and returns to table right.*)

And readin' the papers same as if they was 'ome in their front parlours. Go to bed down here and wake up at Glasgow. Never a thought to the injun what's takin' 'em.

MARY. *(Sitting at table left.)* One takes these things for granted nowadays.

NOAH. *(To* **MARY.***)* Aye. Perhaps the injuns think they've been took for granted too long.

MARY. The engines?

NOAH. Aye, the injuns. *(His manner changes – breaking away centre.)* See here, Miss, 'ow many accidents have there been to mainline trains this past five weeks?

MARY. *(Rising.)* But they say a madman is doing it – Jack the Wrecker people call him.

NOAH. *(Continuing.)* Five in the last five weeks and each one on a Thursday. And to-day's Thursday, too. Ninety-seven men and women killed, some burned to death.

MARY. I know. It's too horrible.

GLADYS. Well, Jack the Wrecker hasn't interfered with *our* line.

NOAH. *(Significantly.)* Not yet.

GLADYS. And Mr. Barney says our traffic returns are going up leaps and bounds. People travel Great Trunk because they think it's safe.

NOAH. There's no sich person as Jack the Wrecker. Never was no sich person. It's the injuns as is doin' it. It ain't natural for folk to travel so soft. God didn't never intend it, and the injuns knows it. Why my fav'rite injun – 'ad 'er scrapped, Sir Gervaise did, just because she shook 'em up a bit – a cruel shame. *(Turning up stage and back again.)* Look at that there big liner – jazz bands, restaurants and all! They said nothin' couldn't never sink her. Nothin'. Not storm, nor sea, not God Hisself! Well, what's happened?

GLADYS. Well, you are a little ray of sunshine!

MILLY. *(Switching on light down right and crossing to left.)* Oh dear, next time I go for my holidays, I shall go by motor 'bus, half fare permits or no.

GLADYS. Or do you think the buses are in it too? *(At desk right.)*

NOAH. *(Moving down right centre.)* Buses! *(Giving a snort of contempt.)* No one's naught to fear from buses as can stand their guts shaken about. All them motor things don't count – *(At door right.)* Why, wimmin can drive 'em! Wimmin!

> *(He goes out right with his tool-kit. A faint noise of the station from below.)*

MARY. What a strange old man.

MILLY. Yes, he is queer, but – *(Shaking her head.)* there may be something. *(At table left.)*

GLADYS. Potty! *(Yawning.)* Well, time's up and the boss will be in in a few minutes. Ventilation. *(Opening the window right – station noise increased.)* Then I'm off to snatch a cup of tea at the refreshment counter on number six platform. *(Going out by the door left.)*

> *(**MARY** is up centre. **MR. BARNEY** enters from the door right. He is a scholastic-looking man, very angular and almost grey. He wears glasses.)*

BARNEY. *(Crossing to left.)* Any telephone message while I've been out? *(At desk left.)*

MILLY. *(Moving to desk left.)* No, Mr. Barney.

BARNEY. Have you finished copying those new sections?

MILLY. Be ready in half an hour, Mr. Barney.

BARNEY. We're terribly behind – *(Frowning.)* at this rate we shan't have the timetable finished by Christmas.

MILLY. There've been so many sections to do again.

(The station noises decrease.)

BARNEY. *(His eyes flashing with rage.)* Because the other companies with whom we make connections will *not* run to time. Losing time on a run ought to be made a criminal offence.

(Train whistles loudly.)

Oh my God! Shut that window, shut that window.

*(**MARY** crosses and does so. The noise decreases.)*

Well, get those new sections done as soon as you can.

MILLY. Yes, Mr. Barney. *(To **MARY**.)* Would you mind reading them out to me?

MARY. Certainly.

MILLY. *(To **MARY**.)* It's quite easy once you got the hang of it.

*(She goes out by door left. **MARY** starts to follow.)*

BARNEY. *(To **MARY**.)* Just a moment, please. *(Tapping desk with, his pencil.)*

(Station noises cease.)

MARY. *(Left centre.)* Yes, Mr. Barney?

BARNEY. Do you realize, young woman, that there are no fewer than three mistakes in those figures? – Three! Arrive Leicester two-fourteen a.m. Leave Hull seven-thirty-eight not seven-fifty-eight. And the one-nine here stops to pick up passengers at Hatchmede on Mondays only.

MARY. I'm very sorry, Mr. Barney.

BARNEY. I was given to understand that you were capable. Miss Baynes was bad enough, but she could distinguish between night and morning. *(Making alteration.)* Two-fourteen a.m.

MARY. I'll see that it doesn't happen again, Mr. Barney.

BARNEY. Yes, do.

MARY. You see, I'm not quite used to this kind of work. When once I settle down –

BARNEY. *(Tapping his desk with his pencil.)* There can be no mistakes in the new timetable. There are enough difficulties already. If you prove inefficient, you go. *(With raised pencil.)*

MARY. But if I –

BARNEY. You go! *(Putting down pencil and taking up sheets and exits by door left.)*

> (**MARY** *watches him smiling, below desk left. There is a knock at the door right.*)

MARY. *(Centre to left.)* Come in.

> (**RATCHETT** *enters.*)

RATCHETT. *(Shaking hands.)* Good evening, Miss Shelton!

MARY. Detective-Inspector Ratchett! I am glad to see you.

RATCHETT. Glad to see you, Miss, and I don't mind telling you that we're mighty glad to work with you again.

MARY. *(With a laugh – shaking hands again and turning to desk left.)* Oh! *(Imitating* **BARNEY**.*)* Just a moment, please! Do you realize, Ratchett, that two men inspecting the boat train are not the equivalent of four? *(Tapping desk with pencil.)*

RATCHETT. I beg your pardon?

MARY. When I 'phoned to you to put on four men I meant four – I was given to understand that you were capable. My last inspector was bad enough, but he could distinguish between two and four.

RATCHETT. Very sorry, Miss, but I thought –

MARY. There can be no mistakes in the timetab – the Great Trunk! *(Tapping on desk with pencil.)* There are enough difficulties already. *(Raising the pencil.)* If you prove inefficient you must go!

RATCHETT. But I –

MARY. You go! *(Putting down pencil.)*

RATCHETT. Very good, Miss. *(Turning to right.)*

*(***MARY*** laughs.)*

MARY. Come back, Inspector. I was only pulling your leg. There's a creature here called Barney, who has just been telling me I'm inefficient.

RATCHETT. You – inefficient?

MARY. I've been giving you a sample – I only hope I didn't look as funny as you did.

RATCHETT. Well, Miss, I was kind of surprised.

MARY. So was I! But seriously, Inspector, we cannot be too careful and in future please don't vary my instructions – four means four.

RATCHETT. Very good, Miss. Now you've got me so scared, I'll have to look at the South Express myself. Tell Sir Gervaise that I'll be back in a few minutes.

    (**BARNEY** *re-enters from left.*)

MARY. Shhh!

RATCHETT. Eh? *(Changing his manner.)*

BARNEY. Now then, Miss Shelton – don't waste time standing about. *(Moving to desk left.)*

    (**RATCHETT** *laughs and exits right.*)

There are five more sheets of the Litchenham extension to be copied.

MARY. *(Going to left.)* Yes, Mr. Barney.

BARNEY. And mind, no mistakes this time.

MARY. I will try, Mr. Barney. *(Exits door down left.)*

    (**BARNEY** *picks up papers and consults map on indicator. He is oblivious to any interruption.* **SIR GERVAISE** *and* **ROGER** *enter from right.* **ROGER** *holds the door open until* **SIR GERVAISE** *takes it from him.* **ROGER** *stands left of him.*)

SIR GERVAISE. *(Entering.)* Yes, that's all very well, Roger, but I wish you'd tell Mason that people are not to be admitted to the downstairs office without a permit.

ROGER. *(Crossing to left.)* Right, I will.

SIR GERVAISE. Good day, Barney. *(Moving to desk right.)*

BARNEY. *(Absorbed in his map.)* Good day. *(Turning quickly.)* Doyle, did you give that parcel to the guard?

ROGER. Yes. *(Left.)*

BARNEY. It was most important!

(**ROGER** *exits by door left.*)

SIR GERVAISE. I've just been cornered by an old lady travelling on the six-fifteen to Bognor. She wanted a written assurance that she will get there safely. And there have been four other people in to-day asking us to guarantee *their* journeys.

BARNEY. Ridiculous! (*At indicator.*)

SIR GERVAISE. I'm not so sure. With all these recent disasters, it shows to what extent the scare is getting on the nerves of the general public. If this sort of thing goes on, people will be afraid to travel by rail at all, and I for one wouldn't blame them.

BARNEY. Why?

SIR GERVAISE. (*Walking backwards and forwards right and left, his hands behind him.*) Being involved in a railway smash isn't a nice thing to contemplate. (*Down left.*) It seems rather a strange thing that the higher we scale towards mechanical perfection the more terrible become the results of mechanical disaster. (*To desk right.*) To be sitting one moment in a comfortable dining car, surrounded by every luxury and then suddenly – chaos – darkness – pinned under a mass of wreckage – God, this fellow is a fiend. (*Sitting at desk right.*)

BARNEY. We've escaped him so far –

SIR GERVAISE. Yes, but none the less we have to realize that our turn may come, and soon.

BARNEY. Impossible! Every inch of our track is watched, every train searched and the drivers and firemen doubled.

SIR GERVAISE. They did all those things on the Mid-Western. I've been chatting at the Club with Sir Peter Mackenzie. It is his opinion that in the Lever Bridge disaster some kind of a bomb was placed in the gas cylinders.

BARNEY. *(Sitting at desk left.)* All our trains are lighted by electricity.

SIR GERVAISE. Yes, I know, but –

> *(A guard's whistle sounds from underneath.)*

She's just starting. *(Turning to window right and opening it. Carriage doors slam below.)* I wonder – *(To left of window right. Engine whistle and a train starts.)* Barney! Barney! Quick! Stop her!

BARNEY. *(Rising.)* Really, Sir Gervaise. Stop her?

SIR GERVAISE. You're *sure* every precaution has been taken?

BARNEY. I am certain.

SIR GERVAISE. Very well. then.

> *(**SIR GERVAISE** back again to window right. Pause – the train goes out. **BARNEY** sits again.)*

Well, there she goes, and with a full load too. God send she gets there.

BARNEY. She lost seven minutes yesterday, so I've had her connected up with the indicator, so we shall know if she keeps good time tonight.

SIR GERVAISE. She's going round the bend by the goods yard. I can just see her rear lights.

> *(An engine whistles away in the distance.)*

Going – going – she's gone. *(Shutting window.)* Is she switched on – now? *(Moving almost reluctantly down from the window and looking up at indicator.)*

> (**BARNEY**, *without speaking, moves to indicator and switches on. The little green light appears and moves slowly along the line on map.* **BARNEY** *to desk again.*)

It's certainly an ingenious thing of yours. I like to feel we're in touch. *(Looking up at the indicator.)* It seems to be working all right. You might make a note of the times the light reaches the various points. Then we can verify it from the running sheet to-morrow.

BARNEY. No need for that at all, Sir Gervaise. I've tested it to fifths of a second. I've sat up for weeks to get the synchronization and I know it's *right. (His eyes gleam with the enthusiasm of the inventor.)* You can't have an accident on that.

SIR GERVAISE. From what you showed me yesterday you've got every factor covered but one.

BARNEY. *(Aggrieved.)* What's that?

SIR GERVAISE. *(Moving across to right of* **BARNEY**.*)* The alarm in case of disaster. You've worked that by theory alone. It can only be *proved* by an accident actually happening. And I hope it's *never* proved. *(Resuming his old position at the window right.)*

> (**MILLY** *re-enters from door left with sheet of paper which she puts on* **BARNEY**'s *desk.*)

MILLY. It's been examined, sir.

BARNEY. Thank you.

> (**MILLY** *exits left again.*)

SIR GERVAISE. *(At window.)* If she smashes –

BARNEY. *What, sir?*

SIR GERVAISE. *(Moving from the window.)* I said "If it smashes!" *(To down right.)*

there's a discrepancy in the timetable announcement of service on train number twenty-one, schedule seven, pages fourteen and twenty-six...

BARNEY. If there's any discrepancy, it's in Richardson's department... we don't make mistakes up here.

CLERK. Quite, sir... but his Lordship points out that the train on which he intended to travel on the twenty-eighth ultimo marked 'h' in italics as halting at the low-level platform at Cawthorp, did not even hesitate at that station and he was therefore obliged to entrain later on a train marked 'r' for refreshments in the timetable, but which carried no service... his Lordship avers that the only refreshment he encountered was a bit of cold turbot, a slab of damp cabbage and a plate of stewed fruit... and...

(**SIR GERVAISE** *moves to left of desk right.*)

SIR GERVAISE. *(Impatiently.)* What is this damn fool talking about?

CLERK. ... Thank you, sir... but... his Lordship –

(**SIR GERVAISE** *back to window.*)

BARNEY. What has this department to do with cold cabbage?

CLERK. Quite, sir, quite... but Mr. Richardson states that your timetable, which clearly indicates here on page twenty-six that trains marked '*d* Saturdays only'; '*h* stops at Cawthorpe'; '*p* first and third class Pullman cars only' and '*r* refreshment car' is at fault... and his Lordship, who is here in person, most upset, sir, and threatening to write to the newspapers, demands an explanation... and Mr. Richardson desires to refer the matter to you... as his Lordship's claim would appear to be against your department...and...

SIR GERVAISE. Oh... for God's sake! *(Moving to centre.)*

CLERK. Quite, sir...

BARNEY. I resent any such suggestion. If there *is* any error it is certainly not *ours*. *(Rising.)* And I shall see Richardson myself about it... will you excuse me, Sir Gervaise?

SIR GERVAISE. I shall see you later though, Barney?

BARNEY. Yes, sir. I shan't be leaving until the indicator shows that the South Express is in.

> *(Crosses to door right, followed by the* **CLERK.** *When* **BARNEY** *has gone out the* **CLERK** *turns to* **SIR GERVAISE.***)*

CLERK. *(To* **SIR GERVAISE.***)* Thank you, sir. *(He goes out right.)*

> *(***SIR GERVAISE** *moves down right, then back up centre, and stands gazing at the indicator – the little green light moves steadily on.)*

NOAH. *(Entering at door right.)* Inspector Ratchett, sir.

> *(***RATCHETT** *enters right.)*

SIR GERVAISE. *(Turning.)* Hullo, Ratchett?

RATCHETT. Good day, sir. *(Up right of desk right.)*

SIR GERVAISE. I'll just have Miss Shelton in. *(Touches bell on desk right.)*

> *(Enter* **MILLY** *from door left.)*

Ask Miss Shelton to come here, please.

MILLY. Yes, Sir Gervaise. *(Exits left.)*

SIR GERVAISE. I suppose there's no doubt about the young lady's capabilities? *(Sitting behind desk right.)*

RATCHETT. *(Right of desk right.)* Not a bit, sir. I've worked with her before.

(Enter **MARY** *from left.)*

MARY. Sir Gervaise – ? *(Crossing to centre.)*

SIR GERVAISE. *(Behind desk right.)* Sit down, Miss Shelton.

> *(***RATCHETT*** moves chair from below desk. She sits below* **SIR GERVAISE** *and left of desk right.)*

Have you settled down here all right?

MARY. Yes, quite!

SIR GERVAISE. None of the others suspect anything?

MARY. I am quite sure they don't.

SIR GERVAISE. Good. I've had a very interesting discussion with Sir Peter Mackenzie of the Mid-Western. He agrees with our theory, Ratchett, that this man – the Wrecker, must have accomplices in the various traffic departments.

RATCHETT. I'm sure of it.

SIR GERVAISE. In the analysis of all these catastrophes it's evident that the man must have an intimate knowledge of the working schedules. Case after case seems to show specialized railway knowledge.

RATCHETT. Yes. That's right, sir.

SIR GERVAISE. *(To* **MARY.***)* That is why I applied to the Commissioner at Scotland Yard for expert assistance, and he was good enough to send you along, Miss Shelton. Your inquiries must start from the innermost core of our organization. Everyone of us must be regarded with suspicion, not excluding myself.

MARY. My duties are to cover the staff, then?

SIR GERVAISE. Yes, of course we may be all wrong. The Wrecker may know nothing of the workings – he may be a person quite outside the railroad, aided by remarkable good luck. It seems incredible that any of the girls in this office, for instance, should be the accomplice.

RATCHETT. I don't trust the women, nowadays.

MARY. *(Cheerfully.)* Leave the girls to me.

SIR GERVAISE. Mr. Barney tells me that your men made a thorough examination of the boat train and the South Express before she started.

RATCHETT. Aye, Sir Gervaise – we did. Raked them over from buffers to tail-lights.

SIR GERVAISE. I'm sure the boat train will be all right – but the South Express though – that's a different matter. I have a pre sentiment – in fact, rather more than a presentiment – *(Turning and looking at the indicator.)* Anyway, there she goes all right, so far.

MARY. *(Looking.)* Oh, is it working – Mr. Barney's indicator?

RATCHETT. Everything will be all right, sir. He won't dare touch us.

SIR GERVAISE. If he does... *(Raising his clenched fist.)*

> *(The picture of* **SIR GERVAISE** *falls from the wall left.)*

(Rising.) My God! What's that?

> *(***MARY** *crosses and picks up the picture, shows it to him. Then* **RATCHETT** *takes it. She goes up left of desk left to centre to right.)*

RATCHETT. Only a picture, sir.

SIR GERVAISE. My picture – presented to me when I became Chairman. Well, I don't so much mind anything happening to *me*.

RATCHETT. You're getting morbid, sir. *(Putting picture on left end of table centre.)*

SIR GERVAISE. I dare say, but when one is playing as risky a game as I am – I could tell you something which might throw considerable light on our problem, but I'm not going to do so – yet.

RATCHETT. *(Centre to left.)* Why not, sir?

SIR GERVAISE. Because I intend to take the full responsibility of my own action. Just now I had to make a very terrible decision about the South Express, that is why, just for the moment I allowed a silly trivial thing, like the falling of a picture, to unsettle me.

RATCHETT. Better case your mind of what's on it, sir.

SIR GERVAISE. No. I'll tell you this much and no more – I think I have a clue as to who this damned scoundrel is.

RATCHETT. *(Very excited.)* Jack the Wrecker?

SIR GERVAISE. Yes.

MARY. And you aren't going to tell us?

SIR GERVAISE. Only this. If the South Express makes her destination safely, I'm wrong. If not – if the blow falls – I think we can get our man.

MARY. You think the express is in danger?

SIR GERVAISE. Perhaps.

MARY. And the people on the train?

SIR GERVAISE. I know. That's the damnable part of it.

*(**MARY** crosses to left centre.)*

Sometimes to save the general situation one has to make a heavy sacrifice. I did not shirk my duty in France and I can't shirk it now. But it's the hell of a strain.

RATCHETT. Sir Gervaise, tell me what you have in mind?

SIR GERVAISE. *(Pointing to the indicator.)* On it goes.

MARY. If you have any evidence –

SIR GERVAISE. I have no evidence at all. For tonight, at any rate, I've got to play this game alone.

MARY. Very well.

> *(A knock is heard at the door right and* **LADY BERYL** *enters with* **CHESTER KYLE**. **BERYL** *is a handsome girl of twenty two and* **KYLE** *a rather saturnine young man about town.)*

BERYL. *(Down right.)* May we come in? *(Moving to right centre.)*

> *(***RATCHETT** *crosses to up right.)*

SIR GERVAISE. *(Moving down centre.)* My dear Beryl – why, of course.

(With a change of manner.) Why, hello, Kyle – it's – why, it's queer that you of all persons should be *here*. *(Staring strangely at him.)*

KYLE. *(Down right, rather taken aback).* Is it? Why?

SIR GERVAISE. Well – I – I – I don't know.

RATCHETT. *(Crossing down to door right.)* I'll be getting on, sir.

SIR GERVAISE. Just a moment, Ratchett. I'll be with you presently.

> *(***RATCHETT** *goes out right.)*

BERYL. Roger said we might come around and see the Company's latest toy.

SIR GERVAISE. Yes, certainly. He can show you himself.

MARY. *(Down left.)* Do you want me any more, Sir Gervaise?

SIR GERVAISE. Tell Mr. Roger Lady Beryl Matchley is here.

MARY. Yes, sir. *(She goes out by the door left.)*

SIR GERVAISE. You'll excuse me, won't you? *(Crossing down and exits right.)*

KYLE. What's up with the old man; he looks queer and why the surprise at seeing me?

    *(***ROGER** *enters from door left.)*

ROGER. *(Centre to left.)* Hello, Beryl.

BERYL. Ah, cheerio Roger!

ROGER. 'Evening. *(Curtly.)*

KYLE. *(Centre to right.)* Your uncle seems a little under the weather this evening. Have you been tossing him for half-sovereigns or what?

ROGER. I hadn't noticed it.

KYLE. We just looked in to see your new gadget and to tell you we're dining at the Mayfair –

BERYL. *(Centre.)* You don't mind, Roger – do you? When you called up to say you couldn't take me I rang up Chester – Chester's so *safe*.

KYLE. Safe? Oh, how terribly depressing that sounds, and I'm depressed enough as it is. *(Up centre.)*

BERYL. That's a cheery start for an evening. *(Up centre.)* Well, Roger, so that's the thingumajig! Mr. Barney told us all about it. *(Up to indicator.)* Look, there's a train moving on it, now, isn't it?

ROGER. Yes – that's the South Express.

BERYL. Does it ring a bell or something when a crash comes?

ROGER. *(Up centre to left drily.)* As a matter of fact it does – *if* a crash comes.

BERYL. And if not I suppose you get your penny back.

ROGER. *(Nettled.)* That's not exactly the idea.

KYLE. If there isn't one I'm pretty sure I shan't get *my* penny back,

BERYL. What do you mean, Chester?

KYLE. I've been buying Great Trunk all this month. I had a hunch that you people would last out longest. Up to now I've done pretty well. *(Down right.)*

ROGER. Our stock has stood up excellently against the slump. I know that.

KYLE. *(Below desk right.)* Because your line's so *safe*, eh, Roger? Great brains in the head office and all that sort of thing. Rugger Internationals sticking on stamps, what? *(Standing, swinging his stick like a golf club.)* However, there's been a curious rumour about the last day or two? *(Centre.)*

BERYL. What sort of a rumour? *(By window left.)*

KYLE. *(Sitting on desk right.)* Oh, the usual lying jade perhaps and perhaps not. Simply this. Jack the Wrecker has been so intrigued by some of your holiday resort posters by eminent artists that he's going to get busy on the Great Trunk.

ROGER. That's all nonsense. How can anybody know? Why no one knows even who the devil is, let alone his plans.

BERYL. I'm terribly thrilled about him. *(Down left.)*

KYLE. Well, anyway, there's a strong rumour in the city – strong enough to make me sell all my Great Trunk stock and a lot more I haven't got at today's price.

BERYL. *(Sitting left.)* Don't be absurd, Chester. You can't sell what you haven't got.

KYLE. True, my child, *but you can sell what you are going to have.* If I sell stock today at today's price I don't deliver it until settling day at the end of the month. If the price drops between then and now I can buy at the end of the month at the lower price and the difference goes into my pocket. Perfectly simple, eh?

BERYL. Then if Great Trunk stocks fall you'll make a hatful?

KYLE. That's it, and if they don't, then I shall be down and out. Exciting, eh? Between ourselves, what would suit me would be a nice juicy hell of a smash on the Great Trunk before next settling day.

BERYL. What fun you men do have. Roger, why don't you take some of Chester's shares or stock, or whatever it is? Then you'll be all right either way.

ROGER. *(Leaning against desk left.)* I'm afraid the idea doesn't appeal to me.

BERYL. Oh, how *dull* you are. Chester, will you let me in for a hundred?

KYLE. Certainly.

*(**ROGER** moves to behind desk left.)*

BERYL. I'll let you have a cheque in the morning. Why, this is just like Monte, only it's red and green ; did your rumour say when the accident was expected?

KYLE. No – that's rather too much to expect – even from a rumour.

BERYL. *(Rising and crossing up centre.)* What a pity. If we only knew the date? We could have a cocktail party up here and watch that thing running against him. Like the electric hare.

(**ROGER** *moving round desk to left.*)

KYLE. Well, he's carrying a hell of a lot of my money. *(Looking at his watch.)* Look, if you really want to go to the fight at the Queen's Hall after dinner, I'd better ring up and make sure of those seats. *(Rising.)*

BERYL. Yes, I'm so terribly primitive – I adore a fight. I don't want to miss any of it.

KYLE. Is there anywhere I can telephone?

ROGER. Yes – in there. *(Moving left with **KYLE**.)*

KYLE. Thanks. *(Going into the little office off door left.)*

BERYL. *(Down centre to left.)* Chuck me a cigarette, Roger.

(**ROGER** *hands her his case – she takes one and throws case on desk left.*)

Thanks. *(Crossing and sitting below desk right.)*

ROGER. *(Centre.)* I say, Beryl, why on earth do you go about with that septic swine?

BERYL. Chester? He amuses me for one thing.

ROGER. And the other.

BERYL. He's the best amateur actor in London and you know I adore the stage. Besides –

ROGER. Well?

BERYL. I asked *you* to take me to the Queen's Hall tonight.

ROGER. I explained to you how it was – we're working late here just now.

BERYL. Why take it so seriously? I'm not sure that I've forgiven you for chucking up your rugger. It was the only thing that lifted you from the commonplace.

ROGER. *(Hurt.)* Thank you.

BERYL. I'm sorry, Roger, but it's true. You're so English, one always knows exactly what you are going to do. You've no imagination.

ROGER. I thought just now when you two were gambling on the chances of a railway smash that I had too much, perhaps.

BERYL. Well, why *not* gamble on it? Somebody may as well make something out of it. I knew Chester had a big deal on of some sort because he promised me a platinum cigarette case if –

ROGER. *(Exasperated.)* Look here, Beryl, I know an engagement doesn't count for very much these days – but –

BERYL. We agreed to go our own ways until we got married.

ROGER. But I do draw the line at your being seen about with that cad. When he was talking about his damned share-peddling just now, it was all I could do to keep my hands off him. *(Moving down right.)*

BERYL. Really, Roger, don't be *too* primitive. *Nobody* makes money nowadays except out of other people's misfortunes. Isn't that what the papers call Big Business?

ROGER. Well, I'm damned if I'll have him make money out of *our* misfortune.

BERYL. I think Chester's very sensible. You stay here and moan about Jack the Wrecker. Chester gets busy thinking how to make money out of him, and personally I think he'll pull it off.

ROGER. Not if I can help it.

BERYL. What are you going to do, Roger? Toss the Wrecker for ends and expect your luck to hold?

ROGER. Who knows?

(**KYLE** *re-enters from door left.*)

KYLE. Seats all right. *(Looking at the indicator.)* What's the news from the course? Great Trunk still running strongly? *(Up centre to left.)*

BERYL. *(Rising and moving to centre.)* Chester, Roger seems to think your little gamble more or less a personal outrage.

KYLE. *(Down centre to left.)* Oh, why?

(**BERYL** *backs to against desk right.*)

ROGER. *(Centre to right.)* If you want to know, I've just been telling Beryl that I think you're a damned swine to make the lives of the travelling public, including women and children, the medium of a Stock Exchange gamble.

KYLE. Did you say damned swine?

ROGER. I did. You're as big a swine as Jack the Wrecker himself – at least *he's* mad.

KYLE. You think he's mad?

ROGER. I do!

KYLE. Well, since you are so hot and bothered about him, why not cut out the melodramatic stuff and catch him? *(Down left.)*

BERYL. *(Between them.)* That's just what I said, Chester.

ROGER. It would give me infinite pleasure to do so, Kyle, if only for the satisfaction of *breaking you*.

KYLE. *(At desk left.)* Thanks. Can I have one of your cigarettes?

(*Helping himself from the case which* **BERYL** *has placed on the desk.*)

BERYL. *(Between them.)* I think you forget, Roger, that I am in with Chester to the extent of a hundred.

ROGER. No, Beryl, I had not forgotten.

BERYL. That sounds rather like a challenge, Roger.

ROGER. Just as you please. *(Moving slightly to right.)*

BERYL. I think all this trouble on the railway has got a little the better of your manners.

KYLE. *(Trying to cross to centre).* Oh, come along. You can talk about that tomorrow.

BERYL. *(Stopping him.)* No, Chester, what I have to say I'll say now. Roger has thrown out a challenge and to make it more exciting, I'll increase the stakes. What's the date?

KYLE. The date – December the third.

BERYL. Roger – I give you till the end of the year – that's four weeks from now. Let's agree to meet here in this office on New Year's Eve.

ROGER. To do what?

BERYL. Catch Jack the Wrecker – and recover your sanity.

KYLE. And if he doesn't?

BERYL. *(Up centre.)* Well, I shall probably marry you, Chester.

KYLE. *(Down left.)* In that case, long live Jack the Wrecker.

> (**SIR GERVAISE** *rushes in right very distraught. He holds a slip of paper in his hand, tries to speak and nearly chokes.*)

SIR GERVAISE. *(Right.)* Roger! – Roger! – From the *Daily Mail* Office. The Wrecker. – Going to get our South Express tonight –

ROGER. What?

SIR GERVAISE. *(Centre to right.)* They had it on the telephone –

> *(**BARNEY** enters on the heels of **SIR GERVAISE**.)*

BARNEY. *(Handing **BARNEY** the paper.)* Read this!

> *(**BARNEY** reads it unmoved.)*

(Right.) Rubbish, this is a practical joke.

SIR GERVAISE. *(Taking the paper again.)* I'm not so sure.

BERYL. *(Pointing to the indicator.)* Look at the light.

> *(They all turn and look at Indicator. A pause.)*

ROGER. *(Up centre.)* What's the matter with it? It's all right.

BERYL. I thought I saw it flicker.

ROGER. What do you make of that, Barney?

BARNEY. Oh, I've seen it do that before – atmospherics.

> *(The light flickers again.)*

BERYL. There it is again.

SIR GERVAISE. Barney, get on the wire and stop the train at all costs.

> *(The light flickers and then goes out.)*

ROGER. My God! Look!

ALL. What?

ROGER. God! The light's gone out.

> *(A pause of three seconds, then the red light appears.)*

BERYL. Oh! *(Moving down to **KYLE**.)*

(A pause of one second then the alarm bell rings.)

SIR GERVAISE. My God, it's too late! She crashed! *(Collapsing on the chair below desk right.)*

ROGER. *(To* **BARNEY.***)* Barney, are you sure your machine couldn't go wrong? A fuse, perhaps.

BARNEY. No.

ROGER. Then I'll get on the traffic office – we must have news –

(Rushing out right.)

SIR GERVAISE. Oh, my God! Oh, my God! I should have stopped her.

BARNEY. You couldn't have stopped her, Sir Gervaise! *(Crossing to front of desk left.)*

*(***MARY*** enters quickly from left.)*

Have *you* heard anything?

MARY. No, sir – Oh, what is it? What's happened?

(Moving up to indicator centre.)

SIR GERVAISE. Something warned me and yet I let her go. I stood there and watched her – women and children –

BERYL. Perhaps it isn't true? *(Down left.)*

SIR GERVAISE. I saw her – go round the curve –

*(***ROGER*** enters quickly from door right.)*

Well? Well? *(Rising.)*

ROGER. *(Right.)* The South Express is wrecked.

SIR GERVAISE. I *knew* it. By Heaven, though, there will be retribution. I've *got* him now.

MARY. Who?

SIR GERVAISE. *(Up at the window right.)* Jack the Wrecker. He's wrecked his last train. I've got my evidence now. Fetch Ratchett. Now I know. Jack the Wrecker is – Oh! *(He pitches forward against left end of desk right, with his hand to his heart.)* Jack the Wrecker is – *(He crumples up and falls up centre.)*

> *(**MARY** kneels behind him. **ROGER** rushes to right of him, kneels.)*

BERYL. What is it? *(Backing down left.)*

KYLE. *(To **BERYL**.)* It's all right. He's had a stroke or something – excitement.

ROGER. He's dead.

BERYL. No! No!

BARNEY. *(Crossing to right.)* I'll get a doctor.

ROGER. He's dead, I tell you.

KYLE. Heart failure, I told you so.

ROGER. No, Kyle, he's been shot. Shot through the heart.

(Rising.) The Wrecker has *murdered* him.

> *(Curtain.)*

ACT TWO

Scene One

(The fireplace is down right. The French window up right centre with balcony outside. The door up left centre, bookcases right and left of the door. The sideboard down left. A table desk, is right centre. A small table above fireplace, and a sofa centre to left, slightly on the oblique, up and down stage. A chair left of the table desk, and armchairs below and above fireplace. The telephone is at top of table desk.)

(See ground plan of Scene.)

(When the curtain rises it is evening and **MARY**, **RATCHETT** *and* **ROGER** *are discovered in the room,* **MARY** *sitting on the lower end of sofa,* **ROGER** *seated centre left of table and* **RATCHETT** *on armchair down right below fireplace. On the table desk there is a teatray, etc., and an ash-tray full of cigarette ends.* **RATCHETT** *gets up and knocks out his pipe in the grate. Speaks.)*

RATCHETT. Well, we don't seem to have got much further, Mr. Doyle!

ROGER. Good Heavens – seven o'clock. We've been talking here for three solid hours.

MARY. Surely not! (**MARY** *has a book in her hands in which she has been taking notes.*)

ROGER. *(Listening to watch.)* We have.

RATCHETT. Then I wish we had more to show for it. This is the hardest thing we've been on, eh, Miss Shelton?

MARY. It's so extensive. Six smashes and six different parts of the country. There's the great difficulty.

ROGER. But we've made *some* progress.

MARY. In one direction only. *(Referring to her notebook.)* We know that your uncle was shot through the window by one of those noiseless automatics they make in America. We know, too, that he was shot by the Wrecker.

ROGER. I suppose we *are* sure of that?

MARY. He knew who the Wrecker was and he told us he was taking a big risk.

ROGER. What's our next move?

RATCHETT. I've got a theory. When the Wrecker gets to work again we ought to have more to go on. Cast your mind back a bit. First of all, he claimed responsibility after the accident. Then, he named the train. Then three weeks ago the train and the night. My theory is that next time we shall have the train, the night and place as well.

ROGER. You think he will grow more reckless?

RATCHETT. I do.

ROGER. Why?

MARY. The criminal's natural vanity, which so often brings about his downfall. There have been dozens of cases of it. Anyway, the more reckless he becomes the easier it should be for us to catch him.

ROGER. And in the meantime – ?

MARY. That's the difficulty. We have to protect the general public. We must beat him next time.

RATCHETT. I am very sorry for one thing, Mr. Doyle. It should never have got into the papers about that bet you had with Mr. Kyle. It should have never been known that you were mixed up in this at all.

ROGER. That wasn't my fault, I assure you.

RATCHETT. It's a pity. Everyone should have thought you'd gone back to your football.

ROGER. I know. I'm afraid the mischief's done. *(Rising and moving left centre.)* It looks as if we should have to lie low and wait for the enemy to make the next move?

MARY. Yes. We've done all we can for the present.

(Paper Boy is heard calling off – "Paper – Evenin' News – Paper.")

ROGER. By Jove! It's the Oxford and Cambridge match today. *(Crossing up to door.)* Hi! Noah!

RATCHETT. Noah? Is the old chap over here, then?

ROGER. *(Returning to above chair centre.)* Yes. He was terriby cut up over my uncle's death. Said he couldn't stand being in the office any longer, and so I fixed him up here.

*(Enter **NOAH** from up left.)*

NOAH. Yes, Mr. Roger? *(Moving down to left of **ROGER**.)*

ROGER. I want to know the football results. Get me a paper.

NOAH. All right. Shan't be more nor twenty minutes.

ROGER. Twenty minutes?

NOAH. It's a tidy step to the station.

ROGER. There's a paper boy shouting outside now.

NOAH. Paper boy? You don't want me to *buy* one?

ROGER. Course I do. Here's the penny.

NOAH. S'truth. *(Crossing up to door.)* I could find half a dozen at the station.

ROGER. I don't want half a dozen. I want one, and quickly.

NOAH. Holy Moses! Buy a paper! Me! *(Exits door up left.)*

RATCHETT. Queer old fellow, that. Deuced queer. Got funny ideas.

MARY. You don't think – ?

RATCHETT. You never know. *(Moving up to table above fire right and picking up his coat, etc.)*

ROGER. Don't waste your time worrying about old Noah. He's been in the company for over forty years.

RATCHETT. That may be, sir, but – *(Shaking his head and beginning to put on his overcoat.)*

ROGER. A drink? *(Crossing to sideboard left.)*

RATCHETT. Not now, sir, thanks all the same. *(Crossing to up centre.)*

*(Enter **NOAH** with paper from up left.)*

NOAH. 'Ere you are then.

ROGER. Thanks, Noah. *(Taking paper and opening it.)*

*(Exit **NOAH**.)*

Here it is. By Jove, a draw!

MARY. A draw?

ROGER. Eleven points each. What a game! Hallo. *(Reading – a pause.)* Well, I'm hanged!

RATCHETT. What is it, sir?

ROGER. Read that. *(Handing him the paper.)*

RATCHETT. *(After reading.)* H'm.

MARY. Well? *(Rising and moving to front of table centre.)*

RATCHETT. This, Miss Shelton. *(Handing her the paper.)*

MARY. *(Reading.)* "Threat to Rugby International. Strange letter to editor. Jack the Wrecker warns Lucky Doyle. Keep out of the way or – ?" So that's why those press men were after you.

RATCHETT. *(Taking paper again.)* Just what I said, sir. All that stuff about that bet – I expected something like this would happen.

ROGER. You don't want me to take that seriously?

RATCHETT. Indeed, I do. *(Putting paper on chair centre.)*

MARY. *(At lower end of sofa.)* You mustn't forget what happened to your uncle.

RATCHETT. Be careful, sir. This is a dangerous man we're up against.

MARY. Ratchett, you'd better get right away to the "Evening News" office and see if you can find out any further details. Get the original letter if you can. *(Crossing and picking up the paper again.)*

RATCHETT. Right, Miss Shelton. I'll go at once.

ROGER. *(Crossing right.)* I've got my car outside, so I'll give you a lift part of the way. I've got to run in to my broker, he's keeping his office open. Will you wait, Miss Shelton? I shan't be more than ten minutes. *(Ringing bell down below fireplace right.)*

MARY. Very well, Mr. Doyle.

ROGER. Come along then, Ratchett. *(Crossing back to up centre.)*

RATCHETT. Only too glad to keep an eye on you.

*(Enter **NOAH**.)*

NOAH. Did I 'ear you ring, Mister Roger? *(Standing between **RATCHETT** and **ROGER**.)*

ROGER. Yes, Noah. It's Jean's night off. Just clear those things away and tell cook I'll have a late supper. Shan't be long, Miss Shelton. Come along, Ratchett.

*(He goes out through the door left with **RATCHETT**.)*

*(**NOAH** down left centre. He eyes the drinks on the sideboard. **MARY** reading the paper.)*

NOAH. So you're going to wait?

MARY. Yes, Noah. Do you mind?

NOAH. No, can't say I do. *(Moving to sideboard and pouring out some whisky.)*

MARY. What are you doing? *(Putting the paper down on the table centre.)*

NOAH. I'm going to drink 'is 'ealth.

MARY. Mr. Doyle's?

NOAH. No, Miss. Poor Sir Jervais-ses. I allus takes 'em in order of seniority – Mister Roger comes later. *(Helping himself to the soda, **MARY** goes to fire, centre.)* What's up, Miss? Anything wrong?

MARY. I'm worried, Noah – very worried.

NOAH. About this 'ere Wrecker chap as don't exist?

MARY. It isn't the Wrecker – it's Mr. Doyle I'm worried about!

NOAH. Ah!

MARY. I want to ask your advice.

NOAH. Ho! *(Crossing to top of sofa.)* Didn't I say all along as you detectives 'ud have to come to me in the end? I'm the only one that knows about injuns.

MARY. Do you *really* believe all you say about the engines?

NOAH. *(By table right centre.)* Listen 'ere, Miss. Up at Fenleton, you know the Railway Works – where they makes injuns – sometimes they turns out half a dozen of the same class. Them injuns are all designed by the same man, all the parts be jist the same – made by the same man. Everything to a thousandth of a ninch. You'd think, then, that them six injuns would be all alike, wouldn't you?

MARY. Of course they are.

NOAH. Well, they ain't. Injuns be as different as folks. One of them runs stady as a rock, another one rolls so bad as they can't run 'er safe at more than thirty-five miles an hour. And yet there be fules what says they're only machines. *(Putting down glass on table centre.)*

MARY. Then you still don't believe in Jack the Wrecker? *(Crossing to below sofa.)*

NOAH. No. There bain't no such chap – I've said so all along.

    *(**MARY** hands him paper.)*

(Reading.) "Blinky Boo the winner of Pe-kin-ese championship."

MARY. No, no, there. *(Close to **NOAH**, pointing to paragraph.)*

NOAH. *(Reading.)* Mister Roger won't take no notice o' that. *(Putting down paper and picking up glass again.)*

MARY. I know. That's why I'm worried. *(Moving slightly to right.)*

NOAH. All wimmin worry too much about the men they love. *(Turning away to left.)*

MARY. What do you mean?

NOAH. Surely, Missy, you don't think as I don't know you're in love with Mister Roger. *(Turning back.)*

MARY. Really, Noah! *(Crossing to fire.)*

NOAH. Don't apologize. I don't mind if you are.

MARY. That's absurd. Why, Mr. Roger is engaged to Lady Beryl Matchley.

NOAH. Maybe. But that don't make no difference to *your* feelings.

MARY. You're quite wrong.

NOAH. *(At sideboard.)* Do you think as a man what knows so much about injuns as I do don't know still more about wimmin? After you've druve an injun like the "Mexboro City" for two years wimmin's just child's play. Deceive yourself if yer like, Miss, but you can't deceive me.

MARY. Oh Noah, what am I going to do? *(Crossing and kneeling on sofa.)*

NOAH. Then I'm right?

MARY. *(Nodding and bowing her head.)* If I thought he'd be happy with Lady Beryl – *(Sitting on sofa.)*

NOAH. Ah, well, I shouldn't worry about that if I were you, if he cares for you –

MARY. Do you think he does?

NOAH. If I was 'im, I know who I'd choose. But no one can't tell really – yet, not till something happens.

MARY. Something happens?

NOAH. Aye, when there's danger, that's when one tells. *(Moving up to left of chair centre.)* That's what set you worrying tonight. That sounds like him coming now.

MARY. Promise me you won't tell him. *(Rising.)*

NOAH. I won't have to tell him – if he can't find out for himself. *(Crossing left to sideboard.)*

(Enter **ROGER**.*)*

ROGER. Back again, Miss Slielton. Hello, Noah, you old scoundrel. After my whisky? *(Right of* **NOAH**.*)*

NOAH. I was just going to drink your 'ealth, Mister Roger. I've drunk Sir Jervais-ses!

ROGER. That's all right, if you don't drink it too deeply.

NOAH. Me and Miss Shelton 'ave just been 'aving a kind of chat. (**MARY** *to below sofa.)* I was telling her that some people round 'ere haven't got no powers of observation –

MARY. Noah! *(Slight move forward.)*

NOAH. It's all right, Miss. I wasn't going to tell him what you said about –

MARY. Noah!!! *(Further move forward.)*

NOAH. Oh all right. *(Exits up left.)*

*(***MARY** *moves to right.)*

ROGER. What's the matter with him? *(Centre.)*

MARY. I – I – don't know. He's a queer old fellow.

ROGER. I have an idea he knows more than we give him credit for.

(He takes out a cigarette, moves to below table centre. **MARY** *eagerly moves to desk, strikes match and lights it for him. Their hands touch, and she, embarrassed, throws match in the grate.)*

MARY. Mr. Doyle, I want you to do me a favour. You mustn't go on with this, it's too dangerous. *(Crossing to right side of sofa.)*

ROGER. Oh, don't you be afraid!

MARY. Mr. Doyle, you misunderstand me. It's not myself I'm afraid for, it's you. *(Below sofa.)*

ROGER. Me? *(To her.)*

MARY. Yes.

ROGER. Why *me?*

MARY. Well, I –

ROGER. Don't worry about me. I can take care of myself.

MARY. Yes – I – I suppose you can. *(Down right.)*

(Enter **NOAH.***)*

NOAH. That there Mr. Kyle. *(Moving to up centre to left.)*

ROGER. Kyle? What the devil – Show him up, Noah.

NOAH. All right. *(Exits up left.)*

ROGER. Kyle, eh?

MARY. In that case I'm going. *(Collecting her hat etc., from the top end of sofa, goes up right centre and cross to up left centre.)*

ROGER. Well, perhaps I had better see him alone. But you'll come back? *(Up centre.)*

MARY. Yes – I – *(To left of* **ROGER.***)*

NOAH. *(Announcing.)* Mr. Kyle. *(Left of door.)*

(Enter **KYLE.***)*

KYLE. *(Standing in the doorway.)* Good evening, Roger. I thought I'd – *(Seeing* **MARY.***)*

(Exit **NOAH.***)*

Hallo! Good evening. Surely we've met – Of course – I remember.

MARY. Good evening.

KYLE. Quite! *(Moving down left.)*

MARY. *(To* **ROGER**.*)* You *will* be careful?

ROGER. *(At door.)* Of course.

    *(***MARY*** exits up left.)*

KYLE. *(Looking after her.)* Pretty kid, that.

ROGER. You ought to be a good judge, Kyle. *(Moving to up centre.)*

KYLE. Oh, it's all right, old man. Don't be nervous, I'm no poacher.

ROGER. Eh?

KYLE. After all, you saw her first.

ROGER. Miss Shelton is here on business.

KYLE. Yes, of course. Yes, to be sure. Aren't you going to give me a drink?

ROGER. *(To above table.)* Help yourself. *(Crossing to fire.)*

    *(***KYLE*** moves to sideboard and takes a drink.)*

I can't say I quite expected you to look in.

KYLE. Didn't you? Why not? I thought that as I was passing – *(Left centre below sofa.)*

ROGER. Good of you.

KYLE. Yes, wasn't it? Here's looking. Oh, aren't you drinking?

ROGER. No thanks. You've struck me at rather a busy moment.

KYLE. After the Wrecker, eh?

ROGER. That's the idea.

KYLE. Poor fellow!

ROGER. Who?

KYLE. Oh, one or the other of you.

ROGER. What?

KYLE. The Wrecker, I mean, of course. I shouldn't like fourteen stone of English Rugger forward on my chest.

ROGER. In that case I hope that *he* won't.

KYLE. Still confident? *(Sitting chair centre.)*

ROGER. Why not?

KYLE. Exactly. With your usual luck. I should like to know how you won the toss in all those Internationals. Was it a double-headed penny?

ROGER. If it was I expect you'd like to buy it. Is that all you've come to ask me?

KYLE. Well – no.

ROGER. I thought so. Which is it this time, then – blackmail, robbery or murder? *(Moving to below table.)*

KYLE. Murder? *(Rising – to **ROGER**.)*

ROGER. *(Putting his cigarette-case on the table.)* Or merely another cigarette?

KYLE. Yes, quite. One up. Thanks.

> *(**KYLE** takes one, lights it. **ROGER** sits on sofa arm down stage.)*

As a matter of fact, though I haven't come here to pull your leg. I know you're surprised to see me ; but I've really come here, Roger, to try and wipe out that little disagreement we had on the night of the smash. *(Sitting centre again.)*

ROGER. Oh!

KYLE. Yes. Look here, Roger, you know this fellow is threatening your life. I have an uneasy feeling that I have been the means of getting you into a nasty position, and I am very sorry about it.

ROGER. Very decent of you.

KYLE. Of course, I know you only went into this Wrecker business because of that silly challenge, and I don't think it's worth the risk.

ROGER. What are you driving at?

KYLE. Well, I suggest we call it all off.

ROGER. What does Beryl say?

KYLE. Beryl? I fancy she'll say the same as I do. She usually does.

ROGER. Very nice – for you.

KYLE. I shall be seeing her later in the evening. Shall I tell her we've agreed to forget it?

ROGER. Tell her just what you like.

KYLE. Then it's all off, eh? And now we're all going to forget about this Wrecker fellow? *(Rising and moving centre to left.)*

ROGER. Oh, so that's it, Kyle? Now I see. *(Rising too.)*

KYLE. What the – ? *(Stopping and turning.)*

ROGER. Do you think I'm a fool? *(To **KYLE**.)* Do you think I don't see that you want to get me off the field because you're afraid I shall catch your friend.

KYLE. But, my dear Roger – you misunderstand – why, he's threatening you.

ROGER. Yes. That shows I'm really getting near him.

KYLE. But –

ROGER. No, it's no good, Kyle. You gambled on a smash on the G.T. The smash came, but in spite of it the stock held up. Now you would like another, because if the stock still keeps up *you go down.*

KYLE. And if there is one, *you* go down, eh?

ROGER. Then you know why G.T. stock held up?

KYLE. Who doesn't?

ROGER. It held up against the smash because I bought Great Trunks with every penny I could lay my hands on. I've sold everything I have. "Why, man, I've even pawned the family Gainsboroughs.

KYLE. You've certainly paid me a compliment.

ROGER. Don't flatter yourself, Kyle. My desire to break you is quite a secondary one. My uncle gave his life for the Great Trunk – I'm his only relative and I'll carry on for the old chap.

KYLE. That sounds beautifully heroic. *(Putting his glass on sideboard.)*

ROGER. Well, you wait.

KYLE. What are you going to do when the next crash comes – sell the carpet? *(Moving to left centre.)*

ROGER. I don't think there will be another crash.

KYLE. How do you know?

ROGER. Because I'm going to catch the Wrecker.

KYLE. If he doesn't catch you first, eh? Well, I must tell Beryl –

ROGER. I think you'd better leave Beryl out of this.

KYLE. I don't think I shall.

ROGER. Then you'd better get out of here before I throw you through that window.

KYLE. Eh? You wouldn't do that?

ROGER. You're quite right – I won't. There's not much credit in bashing a dope-sodden rat like you, Kyle.

KYLE. Damn you, shut up!

ROGER. I'm going to play you at your own game – and to beat you at it, and now – get out.

KYLE. *(With a laugh.)* What fun your barbarian type seems to get out of life. *(Turning up stage.)* Then I'm wasting my time?

ROGER. You're wasting *mine*. *(Crossing down right.)* This happens to be my busy night. *(Ringing bell below fireplace.)*

KYLE. Perhaps you'll be busier still before long. *(Turning near the door.)*

ROGER. I shouldn't wait and see. *(Returning to below table.)*

(Enter NOAH.)

KYLE. No, I don't think I will, thanks awfully. Good-bye. *(At door.)* If you catch your fox save mo the brush.

ROGER. Why? Won't you be in at the kill? Show Mr. Kyle out.

KYLE. Thanks, I can go alone. It's quicker – I'm going to be rather busy too.

(He exits whistling. NOAH is about to follow.)

ROGER. Wait a bit, Noah. *(Moving up centre.)* You know I told you I might be going away?

NOAH. Ah! *(Left centre.)*

ROGER. You remember your instructions?

NOAH. Aye, I'm to stay here and look after the wimmin and if anybody calls I'm to say you're away foot-ballerin'.

ROGER. That's it. *(Telephone rings.* **ROGER** *goes to it, then changes his mind.)* You'd better answer that. *(Crossing to fire.)*

NOAH. *(In phone.)* Hallo! What? Speak up, can't you, eh? Oh, I'm sorry. It's Mister Barney.

ROGER. Barney? *(Crossing to phone and taking receiver.* **NOAH** *moves to left centre.)* Oh, yes. Hallo Barney, what is it? Important? Well – I – Yes, I shall be here for another hour at least. Right you are, come round at once. *(Putting down receiver.)* When Mr. Barney comes bring him right up. *(Sitting at table centre and starting to work.)*

NOAH. *(To door).* All right. *(The door bell rings off.)*

ROGER. What's that? Remember, Noah.

> *(***NOAH*** goes out.* **ROGER** *absorbed in calculation at desk.* **NOAH** *comes back.)*

NOAH. 'Er ladyship has called to see you.

ROGER. But I thought I told you just now – *(Rising.)*

NOAH. I told her, but –

> *(Enter* **BERYL***.)*

BERYL. *(Moving down centre.)* Roger, I must see you. Never mind the instructions you gave to Noah –

> *(***NOAH*** goes out by door left.)*

ROGER. *(Below centre.)* I gave instructions because I'm on a job of work.

BERYL. I know, I know. That's why I simply *had* to come. I've seen the 'Evening New–' – you're in terrible danger. You must stop this foolish business now. I never dreamt you were in earnest.

ROGER. Not even after your delightful challenge, Beryl?

BERYL. I withdraw it, Roger. I'll say you've won, and let it go at that.

ROGER. That won't interest me until I *have* won.

BERYL. But the danger –

ROGER. Between you and me, Beryl, I'm rather sick of that bluff.

BERYL. But suppose it isn't bluff. I've just met Chester and lie assures me it's genuine.

ROGER. How does he know?

BERYL. I don't know, but he does. Chester has a way of finding out things.

ROGER. What a pity he doesn't turn his talents to solving the mystery. Cigarette? *(Offering her cigarette from box on table – and lighting it for her.)*

BERYL. *(Crossing to top of sofa.)* Thanks. I think Chester would like to help you if you asked him. *(Putting her coat on the sofa.)*

ROGER. Yes, I know.

BERYL. He's very upset over his share transactions – they've all gone wrong. The shares didn't go up or down, or whatever it was they ought to have done.

ROGER. Rather a bore for him. All he can do now is to hope for *another* crash. He'll be disappointed.

BERYL. *(Silting on sofa.)* I'm not thinking about the accident – I'm thinking about you. Roger dear, do give the whole thing up.

ROGER. *(Sitting chair centre.)* Did Kyle suggest your coming to see me?

BERYL. Well, yes.

ROGER. I see. Using you to coax me off the track.

BERYL. Don't be absurd.

ROGER. Then what's your real reason for coming here tonight?

BERYL. Can't you see? Because Chester says you're in danger.

ROGER. Chester says. You are always listening to Chester.

BERYL. Don't be silly, Roger. *(Rising.)* Do give this up. Put something in the papers about it and go off to France with the Harlequins.

ROGER. Yes. And keep out of the way until there's been another crash on the railway. And that fellow has a chance of getting out of his Stock Exchange difficulties.

BERYL. But you can't prevent the accidents.

ROGER. There'll be no more accidents if I catch the Wrecker. *(Rising.)*

BERYL. Then you're still going to –

ROGER. *(Centre.)* Three weeks ago this man was just a name. We knew he existed and nothing more. Now he's taking shape – any time now he may be solid enough for me to take by the throat. That's what I'm going to do.

BERYL. *(Centre to right.)* You know who he is?

ROGER. I am making progress. I soon may.

*(**BERYL** gasps.)*

What's the matter? Have you any objections?

BERYL. Not in the least. *(To below desk with her back to him.)* But I think you will fail.

ROGER. Think so, or *hope* so?

BERYL. I didn't say hope so.

ROGER. No, but you *do*. *(Moving to her – and turning her round.)* Now look here, Beryl. It's time for straight talking. You and Chester seem to have got an entirely wrong idea into your heads.

BERYL. And what's that?

ROGER. You both think I'm after the Wrecker, not through any sense of duty to the Great Trunk, but merely because of that silly challenge and bet you made.

BERYL. Silly? You are not very complimentary.

ROGER. I never am. If you want fancy speeches you must ask Kyle for them.

BERYL. I may follow your advice.

ROGER. Very well. Then I'll tell you now whatever happens I shan't ask you to renew our engagement.

BERYL. That's blunt enough.

ROGER. Perhaps. I should expect two things from my wife.

BERYL. Only two?

ROGER. Yes. Sincerity and loyalty. You haven't either.

BERYL. Thank you.

ROGER. You can keep Chester Kyle on a piece of string if you like, but you can't dangle me on the other end. I know he has some rotten scheme on foot, and frankly, I think you are helping him. At least, to the extent of that hundred he let you in for.

BERYL. Hundred? A great deal more than that, Roger. I followed Chester to the extent of putting into Great Trunk stock everything I could get hold of.

ROGER. The swine!

BERYL. Don't blame poor Chester for that – he doesn't even know. But I'm not worried, I'm going to make a fortune. Chester is certain of it.

ROGER. Optimist.

BERYL. He's clever. They say that Chester is going to be a big noise in the city.

ROGER. A big noise. Now I see.

BERYL. See what?

ROGER. That those stories I've heard about you and disbelieved are true. You're a climber, Beryl ; for ever hunting a celebrity. First you were engaged to Martin Enfield – till he was chucked out of Parliament. Then you were engaged to Tracey, the tennis ex-champion. And now *I've* chucked my serious Rugger – I understand –

BERYL. Then if *that's* the way you feel about it, our little episode is ended.

> (**ROGER** *goes to sofa, returns with her coat – holds it out.*)

Is that the polite equivalent of telling me to go to hell, Roger?

(Silence.) Because if it is you needn't strain your politeness to the extent of helping me on with my coat! *(Snatching the coat, and crossing down left with it putting it on.)*

ROGER. *(Centre.)* I'm sorry, Beryl.

BERYL. I don't want your pity. *(To back of sofa left centre.)* If you think I'm going to stop here and he insulted like this you're mistaken.

ROGER. I didn't mean it as an insult.

BERYL. How very reassuring!

ROGER. Then I shan't see you till the New Year's Eve party?

BERYL. Are you stupid enough to think that I'll come to your party?

ROGER. *You* suggested the party.

BERYL. Damn your party, Roger!

> (*Enter* **RATCHETT**. **BERYL** *moving slightly to left.* **RATCHETT** *between and above them.*)

RATCHETT. I beg your pardon, I'm afraid I'm interrupting?

BERYL. Yes you are. (*Crossing up to door.*) And thanks very much.

> (*Exits by the door left.*)

RATCHETT. H'm! Hope I didn't come in at an awkward moment, sir. (*Down left centre.*)

ROGER. As a matter of fact you did, and thanks very much. (*Crossing to* **RATCHETT** *and shaking his hand, then going to desk and taking a cigarette.*)

RATCHETT. Glad everybody is pleased. No luck at the News Office, sir, they wouldn't give me the original letter, and they didn't seem to know anything more about it. I suggest we ask Miss Shelton to see them. The C.I.D. can scare 'em more than the railway police.

ROGER. That's a good idea.

> (*Enter* **NOAH**.)

NOAH. Miss Shelton's back again – with Mr. Barney.

ROGER. Barney too? Good. Show them up.

> (*Exit* **NOAH**. **ROGER** *sits on top arm of sofa –* **RATCHETT** *crosses to him.*)

I'm going to take your advice, Ratchett, and pretend I've lost interest in the Wrecker.

RATCHETT. You are very wise, sir.

ROGER. Now what we are going to do is –

> (*Enter* **NOAH**.)

NOAH. Miss Shelton and Mister Barney.

(They enter from door left. **NOAH** *exits.)*

ROGER. Back again, Miss Shelton? *(Rising.)* How are you, Barney?

BARNEY. Very annoyed. So here you are, Ratchett.

(Down left. **MARY** *crosses to fire.)*

RATCHETT. Anything wrong, sir?

BARNEY. Yes. I must apologize, Doyle, for rushing in so unexpectedly.

ROGER. Unexpectedly? *(Sitting on top arm of sofa again.)* Not unexpectedly, Barney. You rang up and said you were coming.

BARNEY. Rang? Who rang up?

ROGER. You did – not twenty minutes ago.

BARNEY. I didn't ring up.

*(***MARY*** down right – listens.)*

ROGER. But – surely – I recognized your voice.

BARNEY. My voice? *(Pause.)*

ROGER. Queer.

RATCHETT. A bit too queer, sir, I don't like it.

MARY. You *must* be careful.

BARNEY. Once and for all, Ratchett, you must give up this wild goose chase and attend to the affairs of the Great Trunk.

RATCHETT. But – surely – *(Slightly away to left centre.)*

ROGER. What's happened?

BARNEY. There's a strong rumour among the men that this Wrecker fellow is going after our Rainbow Express to-night. *(Crossing to between* **ROGER** *and* **RATCHETT**.*)*

ROGER. To-night?

BARNEY. I've actually had a deputation at the office asking me not to run the train. Naturally, I refused even to discuss the matter. Once we gave in we should be beaten. There wouldn't be a train running on the G.T. in a week.

ROGER. That's right enough. Rather than take off a single train we'll mount a machine gun on every footplate.

BARNEY. I thought you would agree with me.

RATCHETT. The first thing to do is to get the Yard to put through a universal call – to watch every station on the route.

ROGER. Well, then, see that that's done. These rumours must be stopped. If the confidence of our men is shaken our running times will be seriously interfered with. I shall get back to the office, and you'd better come with me.

MARY. Then the Rainbow runs as usual?

BARNEY. Certainly. To the very minute, I hope. Ready, Ratchett?

RATCHETT. Yes, sir.

> *(Exits with* **BARNEY**, *leaving the door open.* **MARY** *is about to follow, when* **ROGER** *detains her.)*

ROGER. *(Rising.)* Would you mind stopping here a moment? *(Following them to door and shutting it.)*

MARY. Certainly. *(Taking off her coat and putting it on sofa.)* If you want me to. *(Crossing to centre.)*

ROGER. I am glad you came back with Barney. *(Down centre to left.)*

MARY. Are you? *(Sitting in chair centre.)*

ROGER. Yes. I've been wanting to thank you for all you've done. *(Left of her.)*

MARY. I'm afraid I haven't done anything. So far we've failed.

ROGER. Not yet. Anyhow, I haven't. I've narrowed it down, and I'm going on with it.

MARY. I hope I can help you. I love working with you.

ROGER. Yes, we've worked so well together. I've never got on with another girl like I have with you.

MARY. We have so much in common.

ROGER. Yes, that's just it.

MARY. At the Office, I mean. *(Rising and going right centre.)*

ROGER. Of course. *(Pause. Moving down left centre, thinking.)*

MARY. What are you thinking?

ROGER. Just wondering when I'm going to see you again. *(Turning to her.)*

MARY. Do you want to?

ROGER. Again *and again.*

MARY. That's very nice of you, but –

ROGER. But what?

MARY. What about Lady Beryl?

ROGER. Lady Beryl?

MARY. You love her, don't you? *(Pause.)* She loves you? No answer? Perhaps no one really knows till something happens.

ROGER. Something happens?

MARY. When there's danger – that's when one tells, isn't it?

ROGER. *(Moving across close to her.)* Is that why you're worried about me?

MARY. Anyone would be. Why, Lady Beryl must be.

ROGER. She's not here.

MARY. Not here, and you in danger?

ROGER. I'm afraid she's in danger.

MARY. I see. Then you *do* love her. *(Crossing down right.)*

ROGER. It's not that – I – I – *(Following.)*

MARY. No – please – I understand –

ROGER. But I can explain.

*(Enter **NOAH** with letter.)*

NOAH. A note by hand. *(Down centre **MARY** goes to fire.)*

ROGER. Thanks. *(Centre. Taking message.)*

*(Exit **NOAH** left.)*

Beryl's writing. *(Opening it.)* Good God!

MARY. What's the matter? What's happened? *(Moving quickly to below desk.)*

ROGER. She's catching the Rainbow. Look at this. *(To **MARY**.)*

MARY. *(Taking letter and reading.)* "Dear Roger, Forgive me for being a pig. I'm motoring North, and shall pick up Rainbow en route and visit my aunt at Harrogate. Will be at your party after all. Beryl."

ROGER. She's catching the Rainbow. And the Rainbow is threatened. *(Crossing down left.)*

MARY. But it was only a *rumour*, so Barney said.

ROGER. I know, but – *(Coming back to centre.)*

MARY. Then stop the Rainbow from running.

ROGER. We can't do that. You heard what Barney said. *(Close to MARY.)* She will have to take her chance. *(Snatching note.)* She doesn't say which road she's taking. I wonder if the person who brought this note knows. *(Crossing towards the door.)* Ring up the Office will you, and ask if Ratchett is back yet? If so hold the line.

MARY. *(Following up centre.)* Yes, Mr. Doyle.

(**ROGER** *goes out of the door left.*)

When there's danger – *(Crossing to phone.)* City two-one-three-eight, please. Great Trunk Office? Miss Shelton speaking. Is Mr. Ratchett there? He's just gone North. You don't know why? Has he heard anything? No? All right! Thank you.

(**ROGER** *re-enters.*)

ROGER. *(Closing door.)* Too late. The messenger has gone.

MARY. So has Mr. Ratchett.

ROGER. What? *(Moving to her left.)*

MARY. Gone North they say. Couldn't you send someone to catch the messenger?

ROGER. No.

MARY. Why not?

ROGER. There's no one to send.

MARY. What do you mean?

ROGER. There's something wrong here. Noah's gone – We're all alone in the house. The back door is shut and bolted. There's a kettle boiling in the kitchen and things cooking. But not a servant. No one.

MARY. What's that noise?

ROGER. I heard nothing.

MARY. Sounds as if *someone* were in the house. There it is again.

ROGER. *(Crossing up to door and opening it.)* There's no light out here. I'll have another look.

MARY. *(Moving quickly to him.)* Don't, Mr. Doyle, please don't.

ROGER. There's nothing to be afraid of.

MARY. You know the warnings you've had. Suppose it's *him*.

ROGER. No such luck, I'm afraid. *(Standing in doorway.)* Stay here, near the telephone, and if anything *should* happen, call the police. *(Starting to go.)*

MARY. Let me come with you – Roger, please.

> (**ROGER** *exits. She stands listening by door, then passes the window and goes down to the fireplace, her back to the window.*)

When there's danger…

> *(A* **MAN**'s *hand appears from left of curtains.)*

(Screams and dashes towards the door.) Roger! Roger!

> (**THE MAN** *enters by the window – he has a mask and cloak on, and is a hunchback, and switches out the light.*)

THE MAN. *(Intercepting her.)* Stop! *(Closing the door.)*

MARY. *(Backing away.)* Who are you? …What do you want? *(Centre.)*

THE MAN. What do you think?

MARY. I – I don't know. *(Terrified, dropping back down right.)*

THE MAN. Just a word with you, Miss Shelton of Scotland Yard. *(Coming to above centre table.)*

MARY. What is it? Why – you – *You're the Wrecker!*

What do you want here? Please go.

THE MAN. Not yet.

MARY. *(Appealingly.)* Don't hurt him. Oh, please.

THE MAN. I have a little message for you, that's all. Tell him – if he *should* come upstairs again to beware. He's irritating me with his meddling, and if he should do it too much – well – *(Taking a paper knife from the table and breaking it.)* Like that.

ROGER. *(Speaking off left.)* All right, Barney, let yourself out, won't you.

THE MAN. *(Backing up towards the window.)* Only a warning, that's all. You won't forget, will you?

> *(He goes out through the window, draws the curtains and disappears over the balcony rail.* **MARY** *stands frozen with terror –* **ROGER** *opens the door.)*

*(***ROGER*** enters and shuts the door.)*

ROGER. *(Moving to centre.)* That was only Barney knocking downstairs, came back for his attaché-case.

MARY. Barney?

ROGER. Why, what's the matter with the light?

MARY. *(Almost hysterical.)* It was – *Mr. Barney* – downstairs – no one else?

ROGER. Yes. Why? Why did you turn out the light. *(Going to window and turning up the lights.)*

MARY. I didn't. *He did. He's* been up here.

ROGER. Barney? Impossible. I've just left him at the front door. *(Returning up to centre.)*

MARY. Not Mr. Barney. Him. The Wrecker. I saw him.

ROGER. Who?

MARY. The Wrecker. *(Pointing to the window.)* He came in there.

ROGER. You saw him?

MARY. Yes, a terrible looking man – a hunchback with awful hands. He went out through the window again.

ROGER. What? *(Rushing to the window.)*

(She follows him. **MARY** *right,* **ROGER** *left of window.)*

By Jove, he must have used that ladder. See? On the ground. *(Coming down stage.)* Damn, if only. I'd come back sooner.

(Three knocks on door.)

Hullo, what's that? *(Crossing to the door.)* It's locked. *(Three knocks again.)* He's still there. I'll get him yet. *(Rattles handle.)* Blast this lock. By Heaven, I won't be beaten. *(Seizes candlestick off of sideboard and smashes out panel of door. Throws open door.)* No one here. *(Standing outside door in the hall.)*

MARY. Look! *(Up centre.)*

ROGER. What?

MARY. There!

(A note is stuck by a knife to the opposite side of the door. **ROGER** *snatches it down.)*

ROGER. What's this? *(Opening note and reading.)* "The Rainbow Express, Pagham Moor Junction, eleven-fifty-five tonight."

MARY. Ratchett was right – time and place.

ROGER. He *is* after the Rainbow. My car's outside.

> (**MARY** *picking up her coat, etc., off sofa.*)

Pagham Moor! Come along, Mary – we'll beat the Wrecker yet –

> *(They dash out of the door left as the curtain falls.)*

Scene Two

(Scene – A signal cabin at Pagham Moor Junction. Facsimile of small lonely cabin. All around right wall, centre wall at back, and left wall are glass windows. The door is down right. Against right wall and above door is a table. Below the windows in back wall are the signal and point levers; five in one set, the signal levers; and a bit apart and to left of these two point levers. On a hanging shelf above these levers are the various signal instruments, bells, etc., and a framed map of the section. In upper left corner a megaphone, a red lantern (lighted) and a red and a green signal flag. One of the windows in upper left wall is hinged to open. Half-way down left wall is a small cabin stove (with fire), its chimney going up to roof. Below stove, against left wall, a stand desk on which is a book for registering times, etc. over this desk is a telephone, and, over this, a clock. In front of stove a small stool. The cabin is dingy and darkly lit by a hanging lamp from centre of roof. The wind whistles and it rains throughout the entire scene.)

(When curtain rises it is about eleven fifteen a.m. on a wet windy night. **ALFRED**, *a young signalman, is sealed on stool finishing a cup of tea and bread. The telephone rings (three short rings). He rises and answers phone. Puts grub basket on floor above desk, tea can on stove.)*

ALFRED. *(At phone.)* 'Ello... Yes, Bill... No, I 'aven't 'eard nothin' ... What? 'Struth! ...round 'ere... Lor' love a duck. No, 'Orace 'asn't come on yet... *I'll* tell 'im... Right ye are, Bill. So long. *(Suddenly.)* 'Ere, I say... Bill...what won the four-thirty? Wot was second and third? 'Ow many runners? ...All right, Bill, so long. *(Replacing the receiver, looking at the clock and taking shoes from under desk and beginning to change, sitting on stool.)*

> *(The door down right opens and* **HORACE SKEET** *enters. He is a weedy-looking man of about 60, very nervous in his manner. He wears a wet overcoat and cap and carries a lunch-tin and basket.)*

What cheer, 'Orace?

SKEET. *(Right.)* 'Evening, Alf. *(Taking off his coat and hat. Hanging them on pegs down right below door.)*

ALFRED. Nasty night. *(Removing his cord-soled shoes.)*

SKEET. *(Crossing to left.)* Comin' down cats and dogs.

ALFRED. Bill's just rung up.

SKEET. 'As 'e? What's amiss? *(Left, putting his grub basket on floor above desk, tea can on stove.)*

ALFRED. Oh nothin' – as yet.

SKEET. What yer mean – nothin' – *as yet*? *(Signing "on" at the register on desk left.)*

ALFRED. There's a message through – they say *'e's* knockin' round 'ere.

SKEET. Who?

ALFRED. Why, this 'ere Wrecker fellow.

SKEET. Gawd! Jack the Wrecker? Round 'ere? *(Crossing to centre to right.)*

ALFRED. Ah!

SKEET. 'Struth! And you jest finished. It would be my bloomin' luck. *(Moving to table right. Removing his collar and tie.)*

ALFRED. *(Putting on boots.)* What yer gettin' windy about, 'Orace?

(Bell tinkles once in signal instrument.)

Hullo, there's the old freighter at last. Set 'em for me, will you, mate?

> *(**SKEET** sets the levers. Signal code 1: (1) They receive 1 beat from A box. **SKEET** then replies 1 beat to A. He receives 3 beets from A. He sends 1 beat to B box. Receives 1 beat from B. Sends 3 beats to B. (A pause.) Receives 3 beats from B. Sends 3 beats to A. He then sets 2 signal levers right.)*

SKEET. *(Coming to centre).* What's Bill's *full* message, Alf?

ALFRED. Only that the Company's got the notion that some-thin' may be on the move in our section o' the line.

SKEET. I don't like it. *(Moving up to table right.)*

ALFRED. Why worry? We know our jobs – jest carry on with it – after all, it's trains this feller is after – not signalmen.

SKEET. Yus – but – I don't like it, Alf. I'm glad I found my old revolver. *(Opening the drawer of the table up right and bringing out a revolver.)*

ALFRED. *(Rising.)* I'm not sure that 'avin' one of them ain't agin the rules. This is a signal-cabin, not a shootin'-gallery. *(Putting his cord-soled shoes on the floor under desk.)*

(A bell rings twice on instruments.)

SKEET. *(Moving to left.).* Agin the rules or not, I'm glad I got it – nice little gun too – I 'ad it as a souvenir over the water.

ALFRED. *(Signing "off" at desk left.)* What, was you in the R.A.M.C.?

> *(Sound of goods train is heard in the distance.* **ALFRED** *turns to find* **SKEET**'s *gun in his face.)*

'Ere, don't point the damn thing at me. *(Crossing down right and putting on his hat and coat.)* Mind what you're doin' of. You're too windy to 'ave one of them about 'ere. Take my tip and put it away.

> *(The freight train passes –* **SKEET** *sets signal levers and touches signal instrument bells. (Signal Code 2: As freight train passes* **SKEET** *sends 2 beats to B box. Then 2 beats to A box. Pushes back his 2 signal levers.)*

(Crossing left, picks up his basket and can.) There she goes. Nothin' to put through now till the Rainbow. *(Going to the door.)* Damn the rain! *(Turning up collar of coat.)* Well, so long, 'Orace, and mind yer don't shoot yer blinkin' 'ead off.

SKEET. *(Centre.)* 'Eere, I say, Alf. Don't go – not yet.

ALFRED. *(Right centre.)* "What's up? Ain't I seed enough o' this blinkin' bird cage for one day? I wants to get down from it.

SKEET. *(Getting cord shoes from under desk, and sitting on stool left changing.)* Yes, I know, mate, but – suppose you spend the night 'ere? It's rainin' like 'ell.

ALFRED. You've got the wind up proper, 'aven't yer?

SKEET. Well, suppose I 'ave? Ain't it bad enough dumped down 'ere in the middle o' the moor all night wi' not a soul to call to without that Wrecker feller 'anging about, too?

ALFRED. You mind your own bizness, 'Orace, and leave the Wrecker to mind 'is. *(Slightly moving to door.)*

SKEET. Yus, that's all very well, but suppose '*is* bisness, and *mine* 'appens to be the same. Go on, Alf, be a mate – I won't forget.

ALFRED. *(Right centre – after a pause.)* Yus – but what'll my ole woman say?

SKEET. You don't know what danger may be lurkin' about.

ALFRED. Yus, and you don't know my ole woman.

SKEET. You only lives 'alf a mile away. Go and tell 'er and then come back. *(Rising and putting his boots under desk.)*

(A bell rings 2 short beats, then 1 beat.)

ALFRED. You're potty, 'Orace, that's what you are. If aught should go amiss, you could ring up ole Bill.

SKEET. *(To window left.)* A blinkin' lot o' good ringin' up ole Bill with that feller cutting me throat. What the 'ell could Bill do?

ALFRED. Dunno, 'e could say 'e was sorry – anyway. I don't see no reason for him to cut your throat.

SKEET. Dare say. But he does a lot o' things as people don't see no reason for and I don't want to be one of 'em. *(Crossing centre.)* Be a proper pal, Alf; run and tell yer missus and get back as soon as yer can.

ALFRED. Oh, all right. 'Struth, I don't know who's the biggest fool – me or you! So long. *(Opening the door – effect of wind blowing in – and exits.)*

SKEET. *(Crossing to door.)* You *will* come back? *(Calling after him.)*

ALFRED. *(Off in distance.)* Yes, if she'll let me.

*(**SKEET** shuts the door. He goes to window and looks after **ALFRED**, looks about and tries to*

whistle "I want to be happy," then he crosses to telephone left and rings.)

SKEET. *(At 'phone.)* Hello, Bill... 'Orace speakin' ... Yes. Oh, I dunno, I jest thought... 'Ow are you, Bill? What? Oh, I thought I'd jest ask...no offence, Bill. No, 'e's gone – but 'e's comin' back, I *'ope*... Eh? What? Gawd. I 'ope 'e ain't round 'ere. All right. So long, Bill. So long, so long. *(Putting up the receiver very regretfully – stepping back and kicking over the bucket.)* 'Struth, I'm all of a tremble! *(Centre.)*

(There is a knock at the door.)

(Snatching revolver from table and going to door.) Who's there? Is that you, Alf?

RATCHETT. *(Outside.)* Where's the blasted latch?

SKEET. *(Holding door-knob in one hand and revolver in the other.)* Who is it?

RATCHETT. What the hell – stop mucking about with the door.

SKEET. 'Ere, I warns yer – I'm armed – I got a revolver –

RATCHETT. Stop fooling, I say, and open the door.

SKEET. If I shoots, I'll shoot to kill.

RATCHETT. D'you know who I am?

SKEET. Yus, I know yer. Leave me alone, I say. 'Ere –

*(The door is pulled open and **RATCHETT** enters, followed by **HAINES**, another plain-clothes man. **SKEET** backs to up left.)*

RATCHETT. *(Right centre.)* You damned fool, stop messing, can't you? Here, give me that gun.

*(**HAINES** down right by door.)*

SKEET. *(Dropping back.)* Who are you? Look 'ere, mate, I'm only a workin' man – I don't mean you no 'arm.

RATCHETT. *(Centre.)* Give me that gun.

SKEET. No, I don't, not till you tell me who you are.

RATCHETT. Ratchett's my name – railway police – now will you drop that thing?

SKEET. 'Ow do I know yore railway police? I only got yore word for it.

RATCHETT. Here you are, then. *(Taking a licence book from his pocket and showing it to* **SKEET**.*)*

    (**SKEET** *looks at it very nervously.*)

Now are you satisfied?

SKEET. Well, I – I dunno. I s'pose it's all right.

RATCHETT. Of course it's all right. Damn it, man, we're here to look after you, and you keep us out in that rain to begin with and look like putting a bullet through us to end with. For God's sake put down that gun. *(Crossing to stove.)*

SKEET. *(Placing revolver on table up right.)* I beg pardon, sir – but I thought if Jack the Wrecker came it 'ud be best to show a brave face.

RATCHETT. Then you'd better leave that one at home! Take off your coat, Haines, you're wet through.

    (**HAINES** *removes coat, shakes and hangs it on peg down right and sits by stove on stool.*)

SKEET. *(Hopefully.)* Are you going to stop 'ere all night? *(To centre right.)*

RATCHETT. I don't know; it all depends. *(Going to* **SKEET**.*)* What's put the breeze up you? Anything happened?

SKEET. No. Do you think anything's *going* to happen?

RATCHETT. I hope so.

SKEET. 'Ope so?

HAINES. Of course. What d'you think we're here for?

SKEET. To look after me – 'e said.

HAINES. So we are – in a way.

SKEET. What d'you mean by "in a way"?

RATCHETT. He means, that our job is to get the Wrecker.

SKEET. Couldn't you get 'im somewhere else?

RATCHETT. *(Sarcastically.)* Oh, just as you like. We might sit outside in the rain and then if he pops in, you could ask him to pop down and see us.

SKEET. What sort of a bloke d'you think 'e is?

HAINES. *(On stool at stove.)* How do we know?

SKEET. If yer don't know what sort 'e is, 'ow can you know it's 'im when you see 'im? They say 'e's a smart one.

RATCHETT. He's got a head on him all right, and he's got pluck. It wants a nerve to calmly say he's going to wreck the Rainbow Express to-night and give time and place as well.

SKEET. What time is 'e going to do it?

RATCHETT. Eleven fifty-five, he says.

SKEET. Why, that's jest the time the express passes 'ere.

RATCHETT. Exactly. That's why *we* are here.

SKEET. You don't mean that *this* is the place? *(Moving to window right.)*

RATCHETT. Not if we can help it.

SKEET. *(Terrified.)* 'Ere, I say. What are you going to do 1 'Ere, I say. *(Turning to right centre.)*

RATCHETT. Don't be a fool – this is a trap!

SKEET. Yus, and I looks like bein' the bit o' cheese.

RATCHETT. Nothing will happen to you – so don't get the wind up about it. It isn't your fault.

SKEET. *(Crossing right and, taking a drink of water from off table.)* No, it's all the fault o' the noospapers. Three thousand quid the 'Tribune' pays to any man losin' 'is wife in a railway smash. Think o' that. Why, yore a damn sight better off dead. Three thousand quid for losin' your ole sorrer and strife.

HAINES. I wouldn't have my wife killed for three *hundred* thousand –

SKEET. 'Ow long you bin married? *(Centre to right.)*

HAINES. Well, as a matter of fact, I'm not married at all.

SKEET. A...h. Ah.

RATCHETT. *(Looking at clock.)* Hullo – she's due in fifteen minutes. "Well, I think I'll have a look along the line. *(Crossing to door.)*

HAINES. *(Rising.)* I'll come with you.

RATCHETT. No. You stay here. Oh, have you got a gun? I came off in such a hurry, I didn't get one from store.

HAINES. Better have mine.

RATCHETT. Never mind, I'll take *this* one – *(Picking up* **SKEET***'s revolver.)*

SKEET. *(Rushing to* **RATCHETT.***)* 'Ere I say. No, yer don't. That's *my* revolver.

RATCHETT. Here, Haines, give him a receipt for it.

SKEET. I don't want no bloomin' receipt; I wants my revolver. If that murderin' bloke got in 'ere, 'twouldn't be no good showin' 'im a receipt. Give me my revolver.

RATCHETT. You've a licence for it, I suppose.

SKEET. Well, you see, I – I – it was like this –

RATCHETT. A job for you here, Haines – no licence for his revolver. In the meantime I'll look after it for you.

SKEET. 'Ere, I say, go easy.

RATCHETT. *(Putting revolver in his pocket.)* I'll be back soon, Haines.

*(Exits centre, taking **SKEET**'s gun.)*

SKEET. *(Looking out of window right.)* Lumme, he's a one, ain't 'e? Eeg'lar serg'n-major. I tell yer 'e 'adn't no right to take my revolver. I'll put my union on to 'im, that's what I'll do.

HAINES. Oh, dry up. *(Strolling up to the levers and fiddles with one of the two at the left.)*

SKEET. *(Turning and seeing him do this.)* Hi! Don't touch them. You ought to know better.

HAINES. *(Playing with the lever.)* What does it do?

SKEET. Leave it be, I say. Do you want to wreck a train?

HAINES. *(Still touching it.)* Would it?

SKEET. You damn fool, if you pull that lever, the next train would run right through the coal siding a hundred yards up there – and over the embankment.

HAINES. Lor'!

SKEET. *Leave it be, I tell you.*

HAINES. *(Desisting.)* Lor', you're jumpy, ain't you?

SKEET. Yes, I may be. I've fair got the 'orrors tonight.

HAINES. If you go getting the horrors you'll be losing your job.

SKEET. And that wouldn't worry me much if I could lose it quick enough. *(Crossing down to door.)* See 'ere – who is that bloke?

HAINES. He told you. Inspector Ratchett, Chief of the Railway Police.

SKEET. 'Ow long 'ave you known 'im?

HAINES. Never met him till tonight. He picked me up at the junction.

SKEET. Well, I don't like 'im. I got a kind o' instink that 'e ain't 'ere for no good.

HAINES. Rubbish. *(Taking a piece of paper from his pocket and twisting it into a spill and stooping over the fire to light his pipe.)* What about opening a window? It's hot in here.

SKEET. *I'm* not hot.

HAINES. Please yourself. Damn this pipe! *(Again he lights it from the fire.)*

> *(A faint smoke issues from the stove –* **HAINES** *coughs, sits on stool by stove – pause – suddenly looks up.)*

SKEET. *(Centre, suddenly – also looking up.)* What's that?

HAINES. What?

SKEET. Listen. *(His left hand on* **HAINES**' *shoulder.)*

HAINES. I don't hear anything.

SKEET. There's someone on the roof. Listen.

HAINES. Rot!

SKEET. There is, I tell you. *(Looking up at the ceiling.)*

HAINES. It's only the rain.

> *(They listen.)*

Well?

SKEET. I could 'ave sworn to it.

HAINES. Look here, you're not going to put the wind up *me. (Wiping his face.)* Whew! This is a stuffy hole. Anything here to drink?

SKEET. Only water. *(Pointing to it on table up right.)*

HAINES. Get me some, will you, I've come over queer.

> (**SKEET** *gets glass of water from right, and brings it to him –* **HAINES**, *quite groggy, drinks it.*)

SKEET. What's the matter with you? Eh?

HAINES. Dunno. I feel a bit off like. That smoke from the stove I think.

SKEET. *(Taking back glass to table right.)* I don't wonder yer feel queer – I bin feelin' rotten myself this last 'alf hour. And then that bloomin' sarg'n-major takin' my revolver jest about put the tin 'at on it.

> *(The smoke still comes from the stove and* **HAINES**' *head begins to nod.)*

(Drinking himself.) Hadn't no right to take it, 'tweren't 'is. *(Looking out of window.)* 'Ow long d'you think it'll be afore 'e's back?

> *(Silence.)*

Eh? *(Turning.)* 'Ere, what's up with you? *(Crossing to* **HAINES**.*)* Hi! Don't be going to sleep, mate.

HAINES. *(Wavering on stool.)* Who's – going – sleep?

SKEET. You are. 'Ere, wake up.

HAINES. Duty – never – sleep – duty.

SKEET. 'Ere, mate, ain't you well?

HAINES. 'Nother drink.

SKEET. *(Rushing for water.)* 'Ere. *(Coming back with a glass.)* Drink this, mate. *(Holding his head and the glass up to his lips.)* 'Ere, I say. For Gawd's sake what's up? 'Ere. *(Taking **HAINES** by the shoulder and shaking him – crossing back up right with glass.)*

> *(Very slowly **HAINES** topples off the stool and lies still – **SKEET** rushes to him – bends over him – feels him.)*

Hi, mate, wake up! My Gawd. 'E's dead. *(Shaking **HAINES**.)* 'Ere, mate. 'Ere, I say. *(Seeing the blue smoke from the fire.)* I've got it, they've gassed 'im. Through the stove. I knew I heard someone on the roof. *(Quickly putting lid on stove and putting a handkerchief to his mouth and backing away centre.)* What am I going to do? Gawd! It'll be *me* next. *(Dashing to the telephone left.)* Bill – Bill... Hi, Bill! They've gassed him. *(Rushing to centre, picking up the stool and facing the door, calling.)* Who's that? Who's there? Who is it? *(Hearing nothing he flings the stool under the table up right and goes back to the 'phone. He rattles at the instrument.)* Bill, I say! ... Gawd, 'e's cut the line! Oh, my Gawd! *(Going back and kneeling over **HAINES**.)* 'Ere, mate. Ten minutes and the Bainbow will be through. Wake up! *(Crossing right.)* Gawd, I got to do *somethin'*. *(Flinging open the door, and calling.)* Help! *(Shutting door and dashing to the window up left, leaning out and shouting.)* Help! Help! Help!

> *(Noiselessly, the door right opens and a be-cloaked black figure enters, bearing a scarf: **SKEET**, who is leaning out of the window, does not see him. The **STRANGER** seizes **SKEET** from behind, hits him on the head and throws the scarf round his neck – struggle, the **STRANGER** covering **SKEET**'s mouth with a cloth in the scarf.)*

Let go. Let go. Help!

(They struggle over to right. The **STRANGER** *forces* **SKEET** *back over the table with the pad on his mouth.* **SKEET**'s *struggles grow less and he collapses with the scarf tied round his face. He falls up right. The* **STRANGER** *ties scarf over his mouth. The* **STRANGER** *then examines* **HAINES** *and then A bell rings – ting. He touches another bell which answers.)*

(Signal Code 3:)

*(***WRECKER** *receives 1 beat from A box. Replies 1 beat to A. Receives 4 beats from A. Sends 1 beat to B box. Receives 1 beat in return. Sends 4 beats to B.)*

(A pause.)

(Receives 4 Beats from B. Send 4 beats to A. He then pulls over the point left which **HAINES** *has already been touching in the previous scene. He then pulls over the 2 signal levers right.)*

(He throws the diagram out of window left. He gives a final glance at **HAINES** *on floor and starts to door. There are footsteps on stairs – he switches lights off and hides behind overcoats hung on wall below the door.)*

(The door is thrown open and **ROGER** *and* **MARY** *enter –* **ROGER** *wears cap and mackintosh.)*

ROGER. *(Moving to right centre.)* Lord, what a ride!

MARY. *(Behind him.)* It was worth it – if we're on time.

ROGER. *(Stepping further in.)* Hullo – I say – anybody here? Who put out the light?

MARY. It was on till a second ago. *(At door.)*

ROGER. That's odd. *(Taking a torch from pocket and flashing it about room and seeing* **HAINES** *on floor by stove.)* Good God! Who's this?

> *(As* **MARY** *comes further into room, following* **ROGER***, the* **STRANGER** *slips out of the door and disappears.)*

Can't you find the switch? *(Bending over* **HAINES'** *body.)*

MARY. Here it is. *(Finding it by door – switches it on – closes door – then sees* **SKEET** *lying up right.)* Oh, see here.

ROGER. *(Turning and rising.)* What? *(Moving up to* **SKEET***.)*

The signalman. There's something doing here right enough.

> *(They bend over* **SKEET** *and remove the scarf.)*

MARY. Is he dead?

ROGER. No. Chloroform. Pretty stiff dose too, by the way he's breathing. Keep his head down and give him some water. *(Taking off coal and cap and flinging them up centre, going to* **HAINES** *again, and kneeling over him.)* Now what about this chap? Who can *he* be?

MARY. *(Administering to* **SKEET***.)* Suppose – he's the Wrecker.

ROGER. *(Examining body.)* If it *is*, he's pretty well out of action. He's *done for. (Rising.)*

MARY. Probably someone's been tampering with the signals.

ROGER. *(Centre.)* Undoubtedly, but I can't tell you what they've done. And there's no chart! *(Crossing to* **SKEET***.)* We've simply got to get this fellow round.

MARY. Look! It's ten to twelve! The "Rainbow" will be here.

ROGER. I know, I know. I must stop her before she gets into the section. *(Crossing to 'phone.)* Hello, hello, hello! He's cut the wires!

MARY. Oh, what can we do?

ROGER. Suppose he's already put the train through.

(A bell rings twice.)

(To instruments.) By God, he has! The 'Rainbow' is in the section!

MARY. What can we do!?

ROGER. Five minutes! We simply must get this fellow round. *(Turning to* **SKEET.***)*

MARY. Yes.

ROGER. Hi, you! Wake up! D'you hear? Come on man, there's danger. Danger! D'you understand? A train in the section. Danger! Danger! *(Moves left centre.)* If only we knew what he'd done.

*(***SKEET*** groans and opens his eyes.)*

MARY. Look, he's coming round!

*(***ROGER*** crosses to* **SKEET***, and lifts him against table.)*

Hurry, hurry, do something. *(She goes to window left.)*

ROGER. Now listen to me, man!

SKEET. I feel ill – I'm ill!

*(***MARY*** crosses back to below* **SKEET.***)*

ROGER. I know, I know. Listen to me. You've been doped. Someone's trying to wreck the Rainbow Express. She's in the section now. Someone's been monkeying with the signals. Do you hear?

SKEET. Eh?

ROGER. *(Shouting.)* Someone's been monkeying with the signals. D'you understand?

SKEET. Signals? You've no right in here – 'gainst the rules.

ROGER. I know, I know. Listen. The Wrecker's after the express. He's tampered with the points. For God's sake pull yourself together and tell me what to do. Are the points all right? Tell me! Tell me!

SKEET. *(Suddenly realizing.)* What? Express, Rainbow, Points? *(Standing supported by them.)* By gosh, he has 1 He's switched her into the coal siding; she'll go right through the 'stop' and over the embankment. Quick!

(**ROGER** *dashes to instruments.*)

I can't see, I can't see! Push back the lever!

ROGER. Yes, yes. But which one?

SKEET. *(Pointing to the two left-hand ones.)* That one!

ROGER. Yes, yes, but which one of them?

SKEET. That one! Quick! *(Falling in a heap again.)*

MARY. Quick!

ROGER. *(To* **SKEET** *again.)* Yes, I know. But which one? Oh, my God! *(Trying to raise* **SKEET.***)*

(An engine whistle is heard in the distance.)

MARY. Listen, she's coming!

ROGER. Two hundred passengers, women and children! Here you, Signalman, which lever, which you fool?

(A second blast of the whistle. The noise of train very faint in the distance.)

MARY. *(Dashing to window left.)* Listen, she's coming!

ROGER. *(Following her.)* By God, you're right!

MARY. The Red lamp! *(Picking it up.)*

ROGER. That's no good. They'll never see it round the bend.

   *(**MARY** rushes to door right.)*

They couldn't stop in time!

MARY. *(At open door.)* Help! Help! *(Rushing back to centre.)* You must take a chance on these then. *(Pointing to levers.)* He said one of these!

ROGER. Yes, but which one? The right or the left?

MARY. Isn't there any way to tell?

ROGER. No, oh, my God!

MARY. Roger, I've got it!

ROGER. What?

MARY. Toss for it! You've always won the toss for England – toss now and win!

   (The sound of the train is fairly close.)

ROGER. No, no, I can't!

MARY. Yes, don't argue, you *must*! Quick, quick! *(Goes to levers.)* Heads this one, tails that!

ROGER. *(Going centre left.)* By God, I'll risk it! *(Spinning a coin in the air.)*

MARY. Quick, she's here!

ROGER. What is it?

MARY. Heads!

ROGER. Heads it is! *(Pushing back the right-hand lever of the two.)*

(Train noise deafening. **MARY** *stops her ears, and shrinks away down right.* **ROGER** *up centre. The engine whistles. The smoke of the engine fills the back windows, followed by the carriage lights.)*

MARY. She's safe! She's safe!

ROGER. Head it was! Etc...

*(***ROGER*** seizes* **MARY** *and sweeps her off her feet in an ecstatic embrace.)*

(Curtain.)

ACT THREE

(Scene. – Same as Act One.)

(Time. – About eleven fifteen p.m., three weeks after Act Two)

(When the curtain rises, the stage is in darkness except for an electric light on Barney's desk. The stage appears to be empty. **MILLY** *enters left from the office.)*

(Note. – **MILLY**'s *bag, gloves and scarf are on centre table.* **GLADYS**'s *hat, coat and bag also on centre table.)*

MILLY. *(Left centre.)* Who's that?

BARNEY. *(Emerging from under right end of his desk.)* Eh? What?

MILLY. *(Screaming.)* Ah! *(Crossing to centre.)* Oh, Mr. Barney, you *did* give me a turn.

BARNEY. I've lost my red pencil. See if you can find it.

MILLY. Let's have a little more light then. *(Switching on the centre light from down right.)*

BARNEY. It rolled under my desk, I think.

*(***MILLY*** crosses up to desk left.)*

(They search for it on their knees. **GLADYS** *enters right and watches them from right centre groping about;* **BARNEY** *looks up and catches her eyes.)*

Please don't stand there staring like an owl, come and help.

GLADYS. *(Right centre,)* What's the matter, sir?

MILLY. Mr. Barney's lost his pencil – the red one. *(Crossing to up centre.)*

GLADYS. *(Crossing to left of the desk.)* Oh! *(Banging things about on his desk.)*

(MILLY hunts on centre table.)

BARNEY. Don't touch those papers. What are you doing?

GLADYS. Looking for your pencil, Mr. Barney.

BARNEY. Then don't look for it there – upsetting my papers – what next! Don't look for it there, I say!

GLADYS. I beg pardon. I thought it best to look for where it was.

BARNEY. Eh?

(A bell begins to toll out the old year.)

GLADYS. *(Showing pencil.)* Here it is!

BARNEY. Oh! *(Taking it.)* Thank you. Thank you. *(Exits by door left.)*

GLADYS. Isn't he a sheik? I thought you were playing bears when I came in. *(Crossing left to her desk and beginning to type.)* This is a cheery New Year's Eve if you like – I don't think – working overtime when everyone's off charlestoning. Look at the time – twenty past eleven – it is the last of it, thank Heaven!

(During this scene MILLY is putting on her scarf and gloves.)

MILLY. Try to be patient, my dear, even if Mr. Barney *is* petulant.

GLADYS. Well, what does he think we are, machines?

MILLY. Do hurry up, or we'll miss the last bus. *(Moving down to **GLADYS**, then back to up right centre.)*

(The bells are heard tolling out the old year.)

GLADYS. Oh, someone will give me a lift – sailors don't care. Oh, listen – *(Rising and putting some papers on the desk left.)* there's that muffled bell again – I wish those beastly ringers would lose their band parts.

MILLY. I don't like it either. *(Standing looking at the floor where **SIR GERVAISE** fell.)*

GLADYS. What are you looking at? What's the matter?

MILLY. Eh? Er – nothing. I was only thinking.

GLADYS. Take my tip and *don't* if it makes you look like a cod's head. *(Moving to her desk again and sitting.)*

MILLY. That muffled bell made me think of poor Sir Gervaise not a month ago. *(Shuddering.)*

GLADYS. I haven't got time to think of anything except old Barney's time-table. Anyway, I'm going to look for an easier job.

(The bell ceases to toll.)

MILLY. Where?

GLADYS. I'm going to be manager and buyer at Greenwich Observatory and rearrange the solar system. *(Rising with sheet of paper, crossing to left centre.)* It'll be kids play after this.

*(**BARNEY** re-enters from door left.)*

BARNEY. *(At door.)* Well? – *Well? (Crossing to desk left.)*

GLADYS. Just finished the Melton section, sir. *(Giving him paper.)*

BARNEY. Thank you.

GLADYS. Beady now, Milly. *(Moving up centre to get hat and coat from the table, where they lay when the scene started.)*

BARNEY. Just a minute, please. You've not finished yet. I want to be sure we have Staylebridge connection all right. We'll check them through.

GLADYS. To-night, sir? *(Up centre.)*

BARNEY. Yes, please. *(Sitting.)*

GLADYS. Oh my God! *(To* **MILLY,** *who is below desk right.)* You run along, my dear, while you're young enough to walk. And you might call at the post office on the way.

MILLY. You want me to phone your mother?

GLADYS. No, I want you to tell 'em to keep my old age pension for me.

MILLY. Gladys! You *are* a one! *(Crossing to door.)* Well – Happy New Year to you. Good night, Mr. Barney. *(Exits door right.)*

BARNEY. Good night. I'm ready now.

GLADYS. *(Making a face.)* Yes, Mr. Barney. *(Taking her notebook and pencil from centre table and the chair from below desk right to right of desk left, and sitting.)*

BARNEY. *(Looking at his papers.)* We'll start with section one hundred and forty-three, I think. *(Giving her a paper.)* Have you got the place?

GLADYS. Yes.

BARNEY. Suttley nine-forty-seven, Wareford nine-fifty-nine, Pond ten-six, Headstone Vale ten-forty-two, Sparling Brook ten-fifty-one, World's End stop.

(**GLADYS** *repeats each name after him. At "World's End"* **GLADYS** *yawns audibly.* **BARNEY** *looks up.*)

Are you attending?

GLADYS. Yes, Mr. Barney.

BARNEY. *(Accusingly.)* Where had I got to?

GLADYS. *(Yawning again.)* World's End.

BARNEY. World's End ten-fifty-seven – that's where we make our connection with the L.M.S. – Now we want –

(*A burst of steam and whistle off.* **BARNEY** *exclaims with irritation.*)

Oh, that noise! Oh! *(Clutching his head.)* Oh, that noise!

GLADYS. What's the matter, Mr. Barney? – What's the matter?

BARNEY. *(Rising.)* Oh, I don't know – somehow to-night I feel – the time-table will never be finished. *(Crossing down right.)*

GLADYS. Oh, Mr. *Barney*! Don't say such upsetting things – and on New Year's Eve too!

BARNEY. Yes, of course it *is* New Year's Eve, isn't it? I was almost forgetting. *(Moving to up centre.)* Mr. Doyle was to catch the Wrecker by to-night, wasn't he?

GLADYS. Yes. He's having a party here to celebrate it.

BARNEY. *(Moving down right again).* He's a lot to answer for, that man; *(Crossing to up centre again.)* if it hadn't been for all these scares I should have had my time-table finished. *(Up centre slightly below* **GLADYS.***)*

GLADYS. *(Rising – to* **BARNEY.***)* I'm sure you would, Mr. Barney – we used to take *such* an interest in it – before –

BARNEY. *(Right of her – eagerly.)* Did you? Yes, I believe you did. It is a great conception, *isn't* it? If only we could eliminate all lost time and make full use of the tracks, do you know what the saving would be?

GLADYS. Oh, pounds and pounds and pounds, I should think.

BARNEY. *(Turning sharply.)* What!

GLADYS. *(Hastily.)* Oh *more* than that.

> *(Turning up laughing – putting notebook, etc., on the desk left.)*
>
> *(Enter **NOAH** right with basket containing champagne bottles, glasses, and a box of cigarettes.)*

BARNEY. What is it, Noah? *(Centre.)*

NOAH. *(Right.)* Mr. Roger's orders, I was to arrange the office for his friends to-night. *(Putting basket on desk right and emptying it of its contents.)*

BARNEY. *(Annoyed).* Friends? What friends?

NOAH. He's a party coming to-night to see the New Year come in at the office. *(Moving chair from table right to below desk right. Putting cigarettes on file-case up right.)*

BARNEY. In that case I'm afraid we can't do any more –

> *(To front of his desk.)*

GLADYS. Can I go home then, Mr. Barney?

BARNEY. Yes, I suppose so. *(Leaning against his desk.)*

GLADYS. Oh, thank you. *(Getting hat and coat from up a. and putting them on.)* You look tired, Mr. Barney – hadn't you better stop working, too? After all, it's New Year's Eve.

(**NOAH** *goes out right for more party requisites.*)

BARNEY. (*Looking up.*) Stop work? No. I'm behindhand as it is – pages behind – (*Moving to back of desk and sitting.*) With all these delays the first sections are already out of date – we've been losing time – losing time.

GLADYS. (*Looking at him kindly.*) I know, but one shouldn't overwork. You haven't had any dinner –

BARNEY. (*Impatiently.*) That will do. (*Resumes working.*)

(**GLADYS** *moves to door.*)

GLADYS. (*Shrugging her shoulders.*) Oh, well – (*At door – gently.*) Goodnight, Mr. Barney – Happy New Year. Barney. Er – Happy New Year.

(*Exit* **GLADYS** *right.*)

(**NOAH** *re-enters with basket of plates. He makes a dreadful clatter with them. He puts them on desk right.*)

Quiet, quiet!

(*More noise from* **NOAH**.)

I'm going out to get something to eat. (*Rising, and crossing down left.*) Don't disturb these papers.

NOAH. (*Crossing centre.*) Papers! No, I'll leave them be.

(*Exit* **BARNEY** *door left.*)

(**NOAH** *is about to open a bottle when* **ROGER** *enters right.*)

ROGER. (*Down right.*) Hullo, Noah! (*Moving to up centre.*) Got everything ready? (*Taking off hat and coat and putting them on table centre.*)

NOAH. *(By left of desk right.)* Aye, Mister Roger, it be all come – champagne, fruit and sich-like – everything save the sandwiches, so I'm 'aving some sent up from the refreshment room – Heaven help you! *(Crossing right.)*

ROGER. Did you get the cigarettes?

NOAH. Yes, sir. There they are. *(On file-case right.)* Seems to me you're wastin' a lot o' time with partying and sich-like.

ROGER. I'm going to get the Wrecker to-night!

NOAH. How can you get hold of what don't exist, Mister Roger? You won't get the injuns to come to no parties.

ROGER. You get on with your job and leave the injins to me!

> *(Moving cigarettes from file-case to desk right. Remaining left of desk right.)*

NOAH. *(Crossing to door right.)* As long as I don't leave you to the injuns, sir. I don't want you to be goin' the same road as Sir Gervaise.

> *(**NOAH** gets to the door just as **MARY** enters in evening dress.)*

*(To **MARY** at door.)* Law me, Miss! In all your falderals! It's good to see you again.

MARY. Thanks, Noah!

> *(**NOAH** exits door right.)*

ROGER. *(Greeting **MARY** – and shaking her hand.)* Ah! Here you are then. Happy New Year.

MARY. It's too early to say that. *(Crossing to centre left.)*

ROGER. *(Centre.)* Then I'm sure of being the first, aren't I?

MARY. It was good of you to ask me to come.

ROGER. It wouldn't be a party without you. And I'm glad you came early.

MARY. You said half-past eleven.

ROGER. I know. I said that particularly. I want everyone to be on time to-night.

MARY. Why particularly?

ROGER. Because of this. *(Taking a paper from pocket, giving it her.)* Telegram. Handed in at Clerkenwell sub-office at eight-thirty this morning.

MARY. *(Reading.)* "Will be with you at midnight." Who's it from?

ROGER. The Wrecker!

MARY. I *can't* believe it.

ROGER. Why not? He kept his last appointment, didn't he?

MARY. At Pagham Moor, yes. But if he comes here – that must be the end.

ROGER. Yes. For one of us! And if I get him it will be thanks to you.

MARY. No. I haven't done very much. *(Putting her cloak on table left, then moving to desk h. and sitting on the left end of it.)*

ROGER. You don't think so? Well *I* do. What about the other night. I should never have had the nerve to toss that coin, if you hadn't thought of it. *(Right of her and quite close.)* And the Rainbow was saved!

MARY. And Lady Beryl was saved. *(Leaning away from him.)*

ROGER. Yes. *(Sitting against the desk right of her.)*

MARY. I'm glad. You've been awfully sweet to me but I know what she means to you.

ROGER. What do you mean?

MARY. I mean – *(Evading it.)* Anyway, if you catch the Wrecker to-night you will have won. Then that will be the end, I suppose?

ROGER. End of what?

MARY. I'm going on a holiday directly this is cleared up. We may not meet again for a long time.

ROGER. But we will meet again. *(Rising and stands right of her.)* Do you think that after all we've gone through together I'm going to let you slip away?

MARY. But Lady Beryl –

ROGER. *(Moving centre.)* It's all off with Lady Beryl.

MARY. But I thought you were engaged to her. *(Rising, and standing left centre.)*

ROGER. Not since the night of Pagham Moor. Before we even started for Pagham Moor.

MARY. Really?

ROGER. Really! *(There is a slight pause.)* Now we are going to settle this business. Come here!

> *(**MARY** looks astonished at his tone of voice, then takes one step towards him.)*

Come here!! *(This is louder still.)*

> *(**MARY** takes another step.)*

MARY. Well?

ROGER. I love you!

MARY. "Oo"!

ROGER. I love you!

MARY. I love you too, Roger. I've loved you all along.

ROGER. *(Moving to her and taking her hand).* Then you're not going away?

MARY. *(Backing away, though her right hand is still held).* I – I need a holiday.

ROGER. Then you'd better make it a honeymoon! You're not going alone.

MARY. *(Pulling her hand away).* Oh! Roger – I know, suppose you toss up for me.

ROGER. Not on your life! I might lose.

>*(**MARY** smiles and **ROGER** sees her.)*

All right, I'll risk it. *(He goes centre.)* Heads you go with me, tails you go alone. *(Tossing the coin, catching it and is about to examine it.)*

MARY. *(Dashing to him.)* NO! Stop! *(Stays his hand.)* I'd die if you lost.

ROGER. *(Laughs – putting coin back in his pocket.)* But I've won!

>*(He is about to kiss her when **RATCHETT** enters right. He carries a small attaché-case.)*

RATCHETT. Good evening.

ROGER. Get out!

>*(**RATCHETT** turns and exits hurriedly.)*

*(Taking **MARY** lightly in his arms and kissing her.)* Happy?

MARY. Terribly happy!

ROGER. All right, Ratchett – you can come in now!

>*(**RATCHETT** re-enters.)*

RATCHETT. Am I to, er – er – *(Beaming with pleasure.)*

ROGER. Yes, you are! *(Releasing her.)*

> *(**MARY** sits at small desk left, **ROGER** turns to **RATCHETT**, who shakes him by the hand.)*

RATCHETT. I congratulate you both.

ROGER. Take off your coat. Well, what's the news?

> *(**RATCHETT** puts his case, hat and coat on centre table.)*

RATCHETT. I'm fair puzzled by the Wrecker's *last* communication. I can't believe it's anything but another practical joke.

ROGER. Well, I believe it's genuine.

RATCHETT. *(Down right centre).* To come *here* – the man himself – it's incredible – why *here?*

ROGER. A lot of people seem to have heard of my New Year's Eve party – why shouldn't he?

MARY. I believe you *know* something.

ROGER. Well, possibly –

RATCHETT. You've discovered the man?

ROGER. I think so, and if my idea is right, the Wrecker will come here to-night of his own accord.

> *(**MARY** rises.)*

I'm banking on that. I'm sure of it!

RATCHETT. Then I'll have the offices surrounded – I'll get on to the Yard.

MARY. I'll help you.

ROGER. Quite unnecessary – Look here, you two. Just leave it to me.

RATCHETT. Not altogether, sir. I'm thinking of your safety and I'm going to do a bit of telephoning. *(Crossing left.) Will* you come with me, Miss Shelton?

> (**MARY** *starts to follow* **RATCHETT** *out door left.)*

MARY. *(At door left – meaningly.)* Yes – I – think I'd better.

ROGER. Here, I say –

(She goes out with **RATCHETT** *left.)*

(Re-reading telegram). "Will be with you at midnight." *(Looking at watch.)* A quarter of an hour and we kick off. *(Crossing to desk left, and standing with his back to audience.)*

> *(The door right opens and a* **MAN** *enters. He is a sinister-looking fellow and keeps one hand threateningly in his jacket pocket as if he had a revolver there.)*

THE MAN. *(Down right.)* Good evening.

ROGER. *(Turning.)* Good evening. What do you want?

THE MAN. I'm looking for a Mr. Roger Doyle. Could you tell me where I'm likely to find him?

ROGER. It all depends. What do you want him for?

THE MAN. I'm afraid I can't tell you. It's an extremely delicate and personal matter.

ROGER. Oh, I see.

THE MAN. *(To right centre.)* Of course I recognize you now. *You* are Mr. Doyle.

ROGER. Suppose I am?

THE MAN. *You* are Mr. Doyle. I have been looking forward to the meeting; in fact I've been trying to get in touch with you for a long time.

ROGER. Well, what about it?

THE MAN. *(Moving to centre.)* Don't you think it was very foolish of you to cross swords with such a desperate man as the Wrecker?

ROGER. I don't see it's any affair of yours.

THE MAN. Pardon me, sir. But it is very much an affair of mine. You know that your life has been threatened?

ROGER. Yes. It's been faintly suggested.

THE MAN. You consider you have had fair warning then?

ROGER. I suppose so.

THE MAN. And you made up your mind to run the risk?

ROGER. Absolutely.

THE MAN. *(Taking a step to him.)* Foolish. Suppose you were to be murdered to-night in this room?

ROGER. Well? *(Backing to desk left.)*

THE MAN. Suppose the Wrecker should come here with a revolver in his pocket, find you unprepared and defenceless and shoot you in cold blood?

ROGER. Well, suppose he did? *(Picks up a heavy ruler from the desk.)*

THE MAN. A ruler would be of little use to you under those circumstances. Put it down, Mr. Doyle.

ROGER. Who the hell are you talking to?

THE MAN. *(Advancing on him.)* To avoid any further misunderstanding, I'll tell you who I am –

ROGER. Yes, and I'll *show you* who I am! *(Making a flying tackle at the man and brings him down centre.)*

THE MAN. What the – ! Help! Let go!

ROGER. Not if I know it? *(Holding the man firmly.)*

THE MAN. Help! Murder! Help! Help! Police!

> *(The door right is flung open and* **CHESTER KYLE** *enters. He is in evening dress.)*

KYLE. *(Down right.)* Here – here! What's all this?

THE MAN. *(Underneath.)* Help! Pull him off! He's killing me!

KYLE. *(Above door right.)* Let him go, Doyle!

ROGER. You keep out of this, Kyle. *(Dragging the man to his feet and props him against the desk right.)* Now then, what's the idea? Out with it. *(Centre.)*

THE MAN. *(Centre right.)* Oh! Let go! I'll have the law on you – unprovoked assault – and me here to do you a good turn. *(Putting his hand into his breast pocket ominously.)*

ROGER. *(Angrily.)* A good turn. Keep your hand out of your pocket!

THE MAN. *(Extracting a card.)* Here's my card. My name's Smith – I represent the Midnight Sun Assurance Company – I knew you were in danger and I only called to suggest that you insure your life.

ROGER. Well, I'm damned.

> *(***ROGER** *and* **KYLE** *laugh.)*

Get out of here!

THE MAN. Our policy has great advantages over all the other –

ROGER. Get out! *(Moving angrily towards him.)*

THE MAN. *(Backing out right.)* The initial premium is only –

ROGER. Get out! *(Following him to door.)*

THE MAN. Certainly. *(At door.)*

ROGER. *(Down right centre.)* And the next time you try this sort of stunt to get a client, you'd better insure your own life first!

THE MAN. Thanks very much. I will. *(Exits door right.)*

KYLE. Sorry if I spoilt your little rough house, Roger.

ROGER. *(Crossing to desk left.)* Not at all. It may serve as a useful pipe-opener when the serious business starts.

KYLE. Then you think the serious business *will* start?

ROGER. Undoubtedly – *and soon.*

KYLE. Excellent. Glad I came.

> *(**RATCHETT** and **MARY** re-enter from door left.)*

Ah! Here comes our sleuthhound.

RATCHETT. *(Crossing to left centre.)* Good evening.

> *(**MARY** down left.)*

(To **ROGER.***)* We got on to the Yard all right, and they'll be sending a couple of men along.

KYLE. Don't let them come in here.

RATCHETT. Why not, sir?

KYLE. Not if you want them to get out alive.

RATCHETT. I don't follow you.

KYLE. *(Putting his coat on table right.)* Ask him. *(Laughing and pointing to* **ROGER.***)*

ROGER. *(Moving to centre.)* I hate to quote old-fashioned proverbs to such a modern person as you are, Kyle, but you may have heard the one about the last laugh.

> *(**RATCHETT** and Mary move to desk left.)*

KYLE. I rather think I'm going to laugh all the time.

(**BERYL** *enters by the door right. She is in evening dress.*)

BERYL. Cheerio everybody. Here we are then!

KYLE. Ah, here comes Beryl. Now I'm sure I am.

BERYL. Am I on time?

KYLE. For once – darling.

BERYL. Evening, Miss Shelton. (*To* **RATCHETT**.) How do you do? (*Crossing to right of* **ROGER**.)

ROGER. Good to see you looking so well, Beryl.

BERYL. Thanks – you're really going to catch the Wrecker man to-night?

ROGER. That was the idea, wasn't it?

BERYL. Before the year was out, you said.

ROGER. That's right.

KYLE. Only seven minutes to go.

(**BARNEY** *enters from left.*)

(*A moment later* **NOAH** *enters from right unobtrusively, and goes up to desk right and arranges glasses, plates, etc.*)

ROGER. That you, Barney? You know all my friends here, I think?

BARNEY. (*Down left, nodding.*) Please excuse me for just a quarter of an hour. I *must* finish this. (*Going to his desk up left and sitting buried in his figures henceforth.*)

ROGER. Oh, sorry.

(*All laugh.*)

(**ROGER** *takes* **BERYL** *up centre to take off her cloak.* **KYLE** *moves up right to join them.*)

Well, what about champagne? *(To left of desk right, joined by* **MARY**.*)* Come along, Mary! Where's that scoundrel Noah?

NOAH. *(Up right.)* I'm here, sir.

ROGER. Well, get a move on and open a bottle.

NOAH. That's one thing I *can't* do, Mister Roger. I can *drink* with one hand, but I can't *open* one.

ROGER. Oh, sorry. *(Turning to* **RATCHETT**.*)* Ratchett, lend a hand, will you?

> *(***RATCHETT*** crosses to above desk right, to* **NOAH** *and opens bottle of champagne.)*

Sit down, Miss Shelton.

> *(***MARY*** sits below the desk right.* **ROGER** *against left corner of desk right.)*

BERYL. *(Moving down to left centre.)* I feel this is going to be awfully thrilling.

KYLE. *(Down centre to left.)* And also very funny.

ROGER. Why funny?

KYLE. I told you just now that I was going to laugh all the time. Shall we tell them, Beryl?

BERYL. If you like.

KYLE. *(Taking her hand.)* Well, Beryl and I were married this morning.

ROGER. The devil you were!

KYLE. *(Holds up* **BERYL***'s hand, showing her ring.)* Is that proof?

ROGER. Not necessarily nowadays – but I'll take your word – if Beryl will endorse it.

> (**KYLE** *crosses up to desk right and takes a sandwich.*)

BERYL. *(Moving to **ROGER**.)* It's true, Roger. Don't be upset. After all, it was you who called off the bet.

ROGER. I'm not upset. I'm laughing too.

> *(Offers her his cigarette-case. She takes a cigarette, turns and lights it from match on desk left.)*

MARY. May *I* laugh too?

ROGER. I think you *ought* to. Come, we'll drink a toast – Noah.

BERYL. No, let's wait till the New Year – then *we* can drink too.

ROGER. Very well – and later on I hope to give you still another chance.

KYLE. *(Moving down right of **ROGER**.)* When you catch the Wrecker?

ROGER. Yes. But there's another still – that's a secret.

KYLE. Oh, well. I've scored – so I don't mind waiting. Even if I am down on your G.T. stock.

ROGER. Serves you damned well right, Kyle. I warned you. *(Crossing to above desk right and getting a drink.)*

KYLE. It doesn't matter. *(Moving over to **BERYL**.)*

ROGER. I should have thought it did. I hear you're stony.

BERYL. Chester!

KYLE. So I am for the moment, but the angel here will provide. *(Taking her hand.)*

ROGER. You are very candid.

KYLE. Why not? Beryl and I have no illusions.

BERYL. *You* have, Chester, if you think *I* will provide. *(Taking her hand away.)* My dear, I haven't a bean!

KYLE. Why, you only had a hundred in.

BERYL. Nearer eight thousand, darling.

KYLE. What!

BERYL. You said you couldn't lose!

KYLE. Well, damn it all, you...

RATCHETT. Sorry to interrupt, Mr. Doyle, but it's one minute to twelve and I'm here to catch the Wrecker.

ROGER. That's easy, Ratchett.

KYLE. We shall see –

ROGER. Kyle, would you consider him "caught" if I have him under lock and key?

KYLE. I suppose so.

ROGER. Good! Mary, will you please lock the door.

*(**MARY** locks the door down right while **ROGER** crosses and locks the door opposite, down left.)*

KYLE. It seems that settles it. You've locked the poor devil out!

*(**RATCHETT**, after looking at his watch, opens the window centre. Sound of sirens, bells, whistles and singing off. **NOAH** hands round glasses of champagne.)*

Listen! Twelve o'clock! A happy New Tear, good people. Noah. Happy New Year! To the injuns!

*(All drink toasts ad lib. during the noise outside. During general noise, **KYLE** moves chair from down right to right of desk right.)*

BARNEY. *(Still seated at his desk, is disturbed by the noise and cries out)*. Oh, stop that noise!

> *(**RATCHETT** shuts the window again.)*
>
> *(When the noise has subsided, **KYLE** continues.)*
>
> *(The bells continue to peal faintly.)*

KYLE. Doyle – a Happy New Year. You've lost!

> *(The positions at the commencement of **KYLE**'s speech are: **NOAH** up centre. **KYLE** down centre. **RATCHETT** below left end of desk right. **BERYL** above desk right. **MARY** up centre. **DOYLE** down centre to left, and **BARNEY** at his desk.)*

ROGER. Same to you, Kyle. But – I've *won*.

MARY. What?

RATCHETT. You've caught the Wrecker?

ROGER. Yes. He's here.

MARY. Where?

RATCHETT. *(Excitedly.)* Here?

ROGER. Steady, Ratchett, please! There's no need to get excited. He's quite safe. He's in this room.

BERYL. What?

KYLE. You mean he's one of us here?

ROGER. *(Quietly.)* I said he's in this room.

BERYL. Then who is it?

ROGER. I'm afraid I can't tell you – yet.

KYLE. Rot! *(Sitting right of the desk right.)*

RATCHETT. Rot be damned, Mr. Kyle! I don't know exactly what game Mr. Doyle's playing, but I'll stand for it no longer.

(The bells cease to peal.)

ROGER. Be quiet, Ratchett!

RATCHETT. No, sir. I've held my tongue too long as it is. I'm tired of all this beating about the bush when all the time I know who the Wrecker is!

MARY. *You* know? *(Down centre.)*

RATCHETT. Yes, I do.

*(**BERYL** moves to below desk right and in between **KYLE** and **RATCHETT**.)*

KYLE. Is this going to be a confession of your own guilt, Inspector?

RATCHETT. *(Angrily.)* No, sir – it's not.

KYLE. Then for the love of Mike tell me!

RATCHETT. Yourself, Mr. Kyle!

*(All exclaim. **ROGER** moves down left.)*

KYLE. This is great! *(Taking a cigarette from his case.)* Has anyone got a match?

RATCHETT. You won't want one, Mr. Kyle. I've got you and you know it!

KYLE. Are you *sure* you've got me?

RATCHETT. I've had my eye on you for a long time. I suspected that you made that bet with Mr. Doyle here and got it all in the papers in order to make your motives so *obvious* that no one could suspect you. That was clever, but it didn't take *me* in.

KYLE. It would take more than *that*!

RATCHETT. Then there was your little Stock Exchange gamble. In consequence of that I had a chat with Sir Rufus Cowan and *he* told me a thing or two I didn't know.

KYLE. I doubt if he found that very difficult.

RATCHETT. Sneer if you like, Mr. Kyle. I've got something more definite than that –

KYLE. Now we're coming to it!

RATCHETT. Yes, we are! Only one person has ever seen the Wrecker – Miss Shelton here – she was nearly scared to death by a man who broke into Mr. Doyle's the night of the attempt on the Rainbow Express.

KYLE. Well?

RATCHETT. That man was you!

MARY. No – I'm sure – it *couldn't* have been!

RATCHETT. It was!

KYLE. Ridiculous –

ROGER. This is a grave charge you're making, Ratchett.

RATCHETT. I know, sir, but I've got my *proof.*

KYLE. *(Rising.)* Proof? Where?

RATCHETT. Here. *(Going up to the table centre and opens his attache-case and taking out a mask, sombrero, cloak. Returning down stage during his speech.)* I found this fancy costume and stuff when I searched your rooms to-night. Now what do you say?

KYLE. You've had the damned impudence to break into my flat?

RATCHETT. I did, and without a warrant –

KYLE. There'll be hell to pay for this.

RATCHETT. You know best. But the game's up.

KYLE. Don't talk like a fool!

RATCHETT. *(Furiously – pointing to cloak, etc.)* In the face of this, do you deny that you were the man Miss Shelton saw in Mr. Doyle's house?

KYLE. No. I admit that.

(**RATCHETT** *moves up centre and puts down clothes on table.*) I was the man!

(**BERYL** *sits below desk right, takes* **KYLE***'s hand.*)

I'm sorry to have scared you, Miss Shelton.

(**MARY** *goes to right of desk left.*)

RATCHETT. *(Coming down left of desk right.)* Enough of that! You'll hang, Mr. Kyle, that's what you'll do.

KYLE. Sorry to disappoint you, Inspector, but I don't think so. A practical joke may be bad form – but I don't think even you can make me – er *(Waving his finger from side to side.)*

RATCHETT. Joke be damned.

KYLE. I entirely agree with you. But I am not the Wrecker, though I admit I have been interested in his activities, and on strictly selfish grounds it suited me that he should not be caught. However, I got a little bored by my friend Doyle's boasting that he would catch this man, and it occurred to me that if *I pretended to be the Wrecker,* for one occasion only, it would probably provide all the excitement he was ever likely to need and he would leave the Wrecker alone and return to his football. Now I hope you are satisfied?

MARY. Then it was you who sent the message that brings us here to-night?

KYLE. No, Miss Shelton. I took up the part of the Wrecker for one night only.

(**MARY** *goes up centre, disgusted.*)

RATCHETT. At any rate, I shall have to take you on suspicion. *(Moving towards* **KYLE**.*)*

> (**BERYL** *intercepts him and he throws her off up stage. She goes to* **MARY** *and* **ROGER** *joins them up centre.*)

KYLE. Oh, no, you won't. *(Putting hand on chair right of desk right.)*

RATCHETT. So you'd better come quietly.

KYLE. On the contrary, it's New Year's Eve and I'll make all the noise I want!

NOAH. Absolutely.

RATCHETT. Oh, we'll see!

KYLE. *(Picking up chair.)* I'll be damned if we'll see!

> (**RATCHETT** *snatches the chair and slams it to the floor.*)

BARNEY. *(Rising.)* Oh, my God! How can anybody work if you people make suck a noise.

RATCHETT. But, Mr. Barney, I've caught the Wrecker!

> *(The positions now are:* **NOAH** *up right.* **KYLE** *down right.* **RATCHETT** *below desk right.* **ROGER** *up centre right.* **MARY** *up centre.* **BERYL** *up centre left.* **BARNEY** *at his desk.)*

KYLE. Oh, don't talk like a fool!

RATCHETT. You can't bluff me – you're my man!

BARNEY. Please! Please! Really it seems to me that there is going to be no peace in this office until we have finished with this Wrecker business. In fact it's become such an intolerable nuisance that there is only one thing left to be done.

ROGER. And what's that, Barney?

BARNEY. I hoped to make some real progress with my timetable to-night, but I see I shall have to put it aside and solve the problem.

RATCHETT. You?

BARNEY. Yes, why not? The matter concerns me as much as anyone else. *(Very methodically blotting his papers, folding them and closing his books. Taking off his glasses then sitting back in his chair and folding his hands.)* Now. How far have you got?

ROGER. Well, Ratchett here accuses Mr. Kyle of being the man we want. Mr. Kyle, while admitting that he meddled in the matter, denies that he is the Wrecker.

BARNEY. Quite so! Mr. Kyle couldn't possibly be the Wrecker.

KYLE. *(To* **RATCHETT.***)* There you are, you see!

RATCHETT. And why not, Mr. Barney?

BARNEY. You have all shown a woeful lack of intelligence. You don't start at the beginning of things – you charge about aimlessly trusting to good fortune. You have overlooked the fact that the man who wrecks the trains is the man who murdered Sir Gervaise – in this very room.

ROGER. That's right enough. Eh, Ratchett?

RATCHETT. Yes.

BARNEY. To accuse Mr. Kyle is sheer waste of time. Sir Gervaise was shot through that window. Mr. Kyle was with us in the room. Therefore Sir Gervaise was certainly not shot by Mr. Kyle so *he* is *not* the man you want. *(Rising and moving round left of desk to centre to left.)*

KYLE. *(To* **RATCHETT.***)* Now I hope you're satisfied.

RATCHETT. I'm not.

BARNEY. The important point is this – who was *not* in the room when Sir Gervaise was murdered? Mr. Kyle was here; Doyle, you were here. Lady Beryl, Miss Shelton, myself. *(To* **NOAH**.*) You* were not in the room.

NOAH. *(A bit tipsy. He has been drinking all during the act.)* Me? No, but I was over in the Railway Arms drinkin' Bill Bank's health.

BARNEY. I make no accusation, I merely state a fact. *(To* **RATCHETT**.*)* Now I come to think of it, Inspector, *you* were not in the room –

RATCHETT. *(Wildly.)* Damn it all, you don't suggest –

KYLE. And why not, Inspector? What a joke if *you* should be *my* man.

BARNEY. Really! Please! Let us keep calm. If we can discover the murderer of Sir Gervaise, then our whole problem is solved. The best and most direct way to do that is to reconstruct the murder. Now you *(To* **NOAH**.*)*, and you, Ratchett, as you were not here, will please stand away.

*(***RATCHETT*** and ***NOAH*** moves up right.)*

Thank you. Now let me see. *(Centre left back to audience.)* You, Lady Beryl, stood over there, Doyle was there, Mr. Kyle here. You, Miss Shelton, were up there.

(They take up the positions: **BARNEY** *down right facing up left.* **MARY** *up centre.* **ROGER** *centre right.* **KYLE** *up left.* **BERYL** *down left.)*

*(***KYLE*** picks up chair thrown by ***RATCHETT*** and puts it above the door left.)*

When I came in through this door Sir Gervaise was standing there. Doyle, perhaps you would be good enough to stand for your uncle.

ROGER. But I went out to telephone after you came in.

BARNEY. And when you came back again, Sir Gervaise was sitting there *(Points to below desk right.)*, wasn't he? And he subsequently went to the window.

ROGER. *(Standing in middle of stage.)* I thought he was here.

BERYL. Must we do this? Let's drop it and play some other game –

BARNEY. Please, Lady Beryl!

BERYL. Well then, I'm going. *(Stepping forward.)*

BARNEY. *(Holding up his hand.)* Please! I don't want *anyone* to leave this room.

KYLE. I don't think my wife should be kept here against her will. In my opinion this scheme of yours is all utter piffle.

BARNEY. On the contrary we shall make definite progress this way. Now, Sir Gervaise was at the window. Will you do that, Doyle. I stood here. *(Crossing to below his desk up left.)*

ROGER. Which window?

BARNEY. That one. *(Indicating window up right.)*

ROGER. Are you sure?

BARNEY. Perfectly.

ROGER. *You* seem more clear about this than I do. Suppose *you* stand for my uncle.

BARNEY. No, I'd rather *you* did. And I'll tell you what to do.

ROGER. *(Not moving).* Well?

BARNEY. Surely it's easy enough. I just want you to move to that window, and assume the position that Sir Gervaise often took up there. You must have noticed his habit.

ROGER. Sorry – but I didn't. But how do you mean? *Show me.*

BARNEY. *(Leaning on his desk.)* He used to stand there, looking out.

ROGER. Oh, I see. *(He steps backwards towards the window right.)*

MARY. *(Screams suddenly.)* Stop! Stop! Don't!

ROGER. Why, what's wrong? *(Left of window right.)*

MARY. *(Vaguely.)* I don't quite know.

> *(There is a pause.)*

BERYL. I've a horrible feeling – as though Sir Gervaise was here again. Noah. Who's to say that he ain't?

> *(Another pause.)*

ROGER. I'm sorry, Barney, I still don't understand exactly what you want.

BARNEY. But – *(Irritably.)* It's perfectly simple. *(Moving to above desk left.)* Sir Gervaise stood at that window.

ROGER. All right. *(Backing to the window right and opening it.)*

> *(As he does so, **BARNEY**'s hand sweeps his papers off his desk – revealing a button which he presses. **ROGER** ducks and a bullet hits a picture on the wall centre behind him, shattering the glass.)*

BERYL. ⎫
MARY. ⎬ *(Together.)* ⎧ *(Screaming.)* Ahh!
⎭ ⎩ Oh! *(Rushing to **ROGER**.)*

> *(**BARNEY** moves chair from right of desk to above the desk between **ROGER** and himself – to act as a barrier, and crouches back against the window.)*

ROGER. *Now* I'll show you how my uncle was murdered. The Wrecker has a gun trained on this window from an empty office across the yard. He fires it by electricity – a button there on that desk. He knew my uncle's habit and killed him. There's your man, Ratchett – *there's the Wrecker! (Pointing to* **BARNEY.***)*

BARNEY. *(Suddenly drawing a revolver.)* Stand back! Stand back, all of you!

> **(ROGER** *pushes* **MARY** *behind him, and* **BERYL** *hides behind* **KYLE.** *All cower back.)*

RATCHETT. God, you're right! He *is* the Wrecker!

BARNEY. Yes, yes! I'm the Wrecker! *(Now completely mad.)* No one is going to meddle with me. Sir Gervaise thought he had me, but I got him first. I was too clever for him! I'm too clever for you all!

KYLE. He's raving mad!

BARNEY. Noise! Trains! Sirens! Steam! Whistles! Noise all round me! How can a man work with his head and whistles, steam and noise all around him. All made by the engines, damn them, the engines that never run to time. Those trains on the other lines – late – our trains had to wait to make the connection – made *them* late – upset all my new time-table – chaos – I killed them – five of them. The South express late three nights running. Three, three, three. I killed it. Do you remember that parcel for the guard, Doyle? That was a bomb and you carried it through this very office. *(A burst of steam off.)* And noise, engines, steam! How could a man work – every damned thing went against me. My time-table would have been great – great
 But the engines – lost time to spite me – noise – late – engines – noise – late – kill them. Kill the trains that lose time! Kill them! Kill them! *(He half collapses against the window.)*

ROGER. Come on, Ratchett. Let's get hold of him.

*(General move towards **BARNEY**.)*

*(**BARNEY** climbs on to bench in front of window, opening the window – flourishing revolver.)*

(All cower back again.)

BARNEY. No, you don't. You can't get me – not yet – I've more work to do – much more – all the trains on the West Coast sections – eight-forty-seven Banbury – Worcester nine-seventeen – Platform three-four-four-four-four!

(There is a sudden blast of a whistle from an engine and the rumble of a train in the distance.)

Ah, the engines – Kill them! Kill them!!

(He throws open the window and springs on to the window-ledge left and disappears.)

RATCHETT. *(Rushing to the window left.)* Damn! He'd fixed & rope. He's pulled it down! Quick! The door! After him!

ROGER. *(Rushing to the door down right.)* The key! The key! Where is it?

MARY. Here's the key! *(Rushing to centre table, getting her bag with the key in it and starting to **ROGER**.)*

KYLE. *(At window left.)* He's safely down! He's crossing the line.

(Noise of train approaching.)

Barney! Barney! Look out!

(Another whistle blast, and the shriek of brakes.)

Oh, my God! My God!

ROGER. What is it? *(The engine noises cease.)*

KYLE. *(Recoiling from window.)* The train! The train! It got him. He didn't see it coming round the bend! Oh, my God! Horrible, horrible! *(Flinging himself into the chair at typist's desk left.)*

> *(**BERYL** crossing to him.)*

NOAH. *(Solemnly.)* Who's to say now it wasn't the "injuns"?

> *(**MARY** moves to **ROGER** down right and huddles against him, his arms around her.)*

> *(Curtain.)*

FURNITURE AND PROPERTY PLOT

ACTS ONE AND THREE

The General Office of the Great Trunk Railway.

Carpet to cover stage.

Rugs at doors right and left.

Table for lady clerk right above door. Chair for same.

Desk up right centre, facing down stage. Chair to same, also chair in front of this desk.

Card index file B.C., B. of this desk.

Long table centre below indicator.

Map of England above indicator.

The indicator is set centre (about 8 feet long by 2⅛ feet high to stand about 2 feet 9 inches from floor).

A little green light appears, and moves slowly along the line on map of the railway. The light flickers twice at cues and then goes out. A pause of 3 seconds, then green lights turn to red. Then alarm bell rings.

Picture of Sir Gervaise is on the wall above type-writing table left, to fall at cue – *If he does.*

Up left centre another desk facing down stage. Lamp to light on same. Waste-paper basket in front of this desk.

Type-writing table with type-writer on same left above door. Chair for same.

Light switch below door right.

Posters and railway pictures about the walls.

Light centre to light the office.

Pens, inkstands, papers, etc., etc., on tables and desks. Blotters, etc.

"Daily Sketch" for Noah.

Apple for Gladys.

Bell to ring off right.

Notebook for Gladys.

Small tool-kit for Noah.

Notebook for Mary.

Red pencil on desk left for Gladys to find.

Deep bell to toll off right.

Cigarettes in case for Doyle.

For Noah, off right, basket containing bottle of champagne and 6 glasses. Box of cigarettes. Basket of plates, etc. Sandwiches in dish.

Attache-case containing mask, sombrero and cloak, for Ratchett.

Revolver for Barney.

Button to press on desk left.

Bullet to hit picture right, glass to break.

Telegram for Roger

Wedding-ring for Beryl.

Matches and trays on desk right and left.

Keys in doors right and left.

Sirens, bells, whistles, hooters, etc., for New Year business.

Train noises, smoke, bells, engine whistles, etc., *off stage*.

ACT TWO

Scene One

The Library of Roger's House.

Carpet.
Fender and fireirons at fireplace B.
Arm-chairs above and below fireplace.
Hearthrug.
Table-desk, small chair at same.
Sofa.
Table, small, above fireplace.
2 bookcases, right and left of door up left.
Door up right (top panel to smash from inside room with candlestick from sideboard).
Sideboard. Pair of silver candlesticks on same. Whisky in decanter, syphon of soda, glasses.
Ash-trays on desk and mantelpiece.
Matches on same and sideboard.
French window, balcony outside same.
Heavy curtains with pelmet to draw.
Light switch left of French window.
Evening newspaper *off* left.
Pipe for Ratchett.
Tea-things on desk (tea is finished).
Telephone top of desk.
Cushions on sofa.
Coins for Doyle.
Cigarette, box of, on desk.
Case of cigarettes for Doyle.
Bell-push below fireplace.
Mask, sombrero, cloak for Kyle.
Note to stick (outside door) to door with knife.
Paper-knife on desk to break.

Scene Two

The Signal Box.

Table up right.
Hat-pegs below door right.
4 telegraphic indicators centre.
Chart of signals.
Bell to ring.
11 levers for signals centre.
Store left about a yard and a half from wall.
Stool in front of stove.
High standing desk down left.
Telephone slightly above desk.
Book for signing-on and off. Papers, pens, ink, etc., on same.
Food basket and tea can for Alfred.
Food basket and tea can for Skeet.
Glass and bottle of water on table up right.
Soft shoes for Alfred and Skeet.
Smoke to work from stove at cue.
Revolver for Skeet.
Train effects: coming nearer and nearer and rushing by signal box. Goods train and express to follow.
Rain effects: to open Scene.
Rain continues, violent at times.
Torchlight for Doyle.
Electric bell to ring as from next signal-box.
Coin for Doyle.
Lantern for Mary (red light). Train noise for finish of the Act.

LIGHTING PLOT

ACT ONE

The General Office of the Great Trunk Railway.

Two large windows are set diagonally right and left. Behind these (are looking down on the London Terminus) signals red and green and yellow are seen. Smoke effects of trains coming in and going out.

The Light is not good in the room when the Scene opens.

Time – 3.30, Afternoon.

Floats and battens down to ¼ (amber).

Red in from centre of floats.

Perches off to open scene.

When lamps are turned up open limes on right and left desks.

Light-switch is down right.

Table lamp to light on desk up left.

Centre light in ceiling to light room.

Trick lights in indicator centre to work to cue.

Green to travel very slowly along railway map of main line. Flicker at cues. Then red to come on in place of green. Then go out and alarm bell to ring.

Light up at cue and out at cue.

Strips (deep amber) outside doors right and left.

ACT II
Scene One

Roger Doyle's *Library*.

Floats and battens (amber). Full up.
Lights to work from switch up left centre by window.
Fire lighted. Red flood from same to settee left centre.
Strip (amber) outside door up left.
Flood outside window on backing (blue).
All lights except backing flood, and strip outside door and fire – off at cue and on again at cue.

Scene Two

The Signal Box.

Floats and battens down to ¼ (deep amber).

Black outside windows.

Rain effects – to open.

Fire in stove and to get smoke effect at cue.

Centre light, one globe.

Perches (deep amber) on to signals centre and stove and seat.

Lights to flash outside windows of box as goods train passes for finish of scene and plenty of flash lighting as Express passes.

www.ingramcontent.com/pod-product-compliance
Ingram Content Group UK Ltd.
Pitfield, Milton Keynes, MK11 3LW, UK
UKHW021839210426
5322IPUK00022B/371